ALSO BY THE AUTHOR

THE
BEST
ADVICE EVER GIVEN

New and Updated—the greatest life
lessons for success in the real world!

Edited and with an introduction by
STEVEN D. PRICE
Revised by Tom McCarthy

Guilford, Connecticut

An imprint of The Rowman & Littlefield Publishing Group, Inc.
4501 Forbes Blvd., Ste. 200
Lanham, MD 20706

Distributed by NATIONAL BOOK NETWORK

British Library Cataloguing in Publication Information Available

Library of Congress Cataloging-in-Publication Data

Names: Price, Steven D., editor. | McCarthy, Tom, 1952- editor.
Title: The best advice ever given : the greatest life lessons for success in
    the real world! / edited and with an introduction by Steven D. Price ;
    revised by Tom McCarthy.
Description: New and updated [edition]. | Guilford, Connecticut : Lyons
    Press, [2018] | Includes bibliographical references and index.
Identifiers: LCCN 2017052726 (print) | LCCN 2017048619 (ebook) | ISBN
    9781493033799 (e-book) | ISBN 9781493033782 (pbk. : alk. paper)
Subjects: LCSH: Life skills—Handbooks, manuals, etc. | Success—Handbooks,
    manuals, etc. | Success—Quotations, maxims, etc. | Quotations.
Classification: LCC HQ2037 (print) | LCC HQ2037 .B47 2018 (ebook) | DDC
    646.7—dc23
LC record available at https://lccn.loc.gov/2017052726

CONTENTS

INTRODUCTION

Advice? Who needs it?

Apparently everyone, because we're bombarded with it throughout our lives. The deluge begins with such dire parental warnings as, "If you don't wear your galoshes, you'll catch your death of cold!" and "Be careful or you'll poke your eye out!" *Aesop's Fables* and cautionary fairy tales introduce us to countless other moral messages. Whatever one's faith, religious education focuses on some form of the "Do unto others" Golden Rule. High school and college literature courses include Polonius's time-worn "to thine own self be true" catalog of counsel in *Hamlet,* and *David Copperfield's* Mr. Micawber and his classic "Annual income twenty pounds . . ." explanation of financial planning. And just when we thought we were finished with faculty advisors and guidance counselors, graduation speakers send us on our way with their advice for getting ahead.

Opinions are everywhere. Got a medical problem? Doctors will dispense advice along with pills. A legal problem? Lawyers are in the business of providing counsel, which is why they're referred to as counselors. Newspaper columnists such as "Dear Abby" and "Miss Manners" include advice in print. Religious leaders, infomercials, and television hosts like Oprah and Dr. Phil do so over the airwaves. Along with every other sort of information, the Internet is advice-rich in all manner of subjects. And throughout our lives, friends and relatives share wisdom and experience of varying degrees of usefulness that begin with a knowing nod and an "I'm going to give you a piece of advice . . . "

How we accept advice depends on what it is and by whom and how it's given. Much of the time we brush it off, because as a New England proverb suggests, "Advice would always be more acceptable if it didn't conflict with our plans." Or we run in the other direction—as the actress Marie Dressler (older readers will remember her as "Tugboat Annie") snapped, "No vice is so bad as advice." Confusing the situation is the abundance of contradictory advice, of the "absence-makes-the-heart-grow-fonder" variety versus "Out of sight, out of mind."

On the other hand, sound advice is not only tolerable, it's welcome. First of all, it tends to be terse—a volume of wisdom in a sentence or two—which is both appealing and expected in this sound-byte age. More important, it sets our feet on the right path; who indeed would want to disregard the global positioning that moral or practical compasses can give? That's what you'll find in this book. Included is advice on education ("Formal education will make you a living. Self-education will make you a fortune." —Jim Rohn), life and living ("Don't carry a grudge. While you're carrying the grudge, the other guy's out dancing." —Buddy Hackett), and success of a personal and financial nature ("You can have it all. You just can't have it all at one time." —Oprah Winfrey).

Also represented here are both romantic and platonic love and friendship ("Immature love says: 'I love you because I need you.' Mature love says: 'I need you because I love you.'" —Erich Fromm), inspiration ("If you can dream it, you can do it." —Walt Disney), and creativity and the arts ("Take the best that exists and make it better. If it doesn't exist, create it." —Sir Henry Royce).

Sports and competition weigh in ("One hundred percent of shots not taken don't go in." —Wayne Gretzky), as do business and leadership

("If two men on the same job agree all the time, then one is unnecessary. If they disagree all the time, then both are useless." —Darryl Zanuck), and proverbs and folk sayings ("If you chase two rabbits, both will escape." —Spanish saying). And if you're not wise enough by then, the book concludes with—of all things—advice about advice ("Don't take a butcher's advice on how to cook meat. If he knew, he'd be a chef." —Andy Rooney).

Readers of my earlier compilations have asked which quotations were my favorites. In the event the same question occurs to you here, my answer remains the same: It depends. When I'm in good spirits or feeling sentimental, any of the warm, fuzzy quotations resonate, such as the bit of cowboy wisdom that points out, "The best sermons are lived, not preached." But if I'm in a dour mood, especially after watching the nightly news' cataclysmic chronicles of human folly and disaster, Damon Runyon's observation that "All life is six to five against" makes an eminently good way to view the world. Another question I've been asked is, "Are these really the best? Aren't there others?" Here the answer can be more definite: I think so, and yes. The quotations you'll find in this book cover all aspects of human existence, including life itself. Certainly there are others, and many have indeed been perceptively expressed or elegantly phrased, but whatever their subjects might be, you'll find them covered in these pages. (I also excluded commandments and orders, which are distinguished from advice by their implied or expressed threat of punishment if disobeyed.)

Many people contributed their favorite quotations and sources in the course of this compilation's creation, for who can refuse the request to "tell me some good advice"? I offer them all my heartfelt thanks.

Chapter One

■ ■ ■ ■ ■ ■ ■ ■ ■

Let Others Light Their Candles

{Advice on a Proper Education}

"One child, one teacher, one book, one pen can change the world."
—MALALA YOUSAFZAI

If you have knowledge, let others light their candles in it.
—MARGARET FULLER

"Try to learn something about everything
and everything about something."
—THOMAS HENRY HUXLEY

In youth we learn; in age we understand.

—MARIE VON EBNER-ESCHENBACH

Learn as though you would never be able to master it;

hold it as though you would be in fear of losing it.

—CONFUCIUS

"Ignorance is not a virtue."

—BARACK OBAMA

Education is only the ladder with which to gather fruit

from the tree of knowledge, not the fruit itself.

—ANONYMOUS

Those who cannot learn from history are doomed to repeat it.
—GEORGE SANTAYANA

•

Never seem wiser, nor more learned, than the people you are with.
Wear your learning, like your watch, in a private pocket, and do not
merely pull it out and strike it merely to show that you have one.
—LORD CHESTERFIELD

•

Education is the passport to the future, for tomorrow
belongs to those who prepare for it today.
—MALCOLM X

"It's important to watch what you put in your mind."
—**LINDA KNIGHT**

Study as if you were going to live forever;

live as if you were going to die tomorrow.
—**MARIA MITCHELL**

Never help a child with a task at which he feels he can succeed.
—**MARIA MONTESSORI**

The man who does not read good books
has no advantage over the man who cannot read them.
—MARK TWAIN

An investment in knowledge pays the best interest.
—BENJAMIN FRANKLIN

"We cannot hold a torch to light another's
path without brightening our own."
—BEN SWEETLAND

Trust should be the basis for all our moral training.
—SIR ROBERT BADEN-POWELL

•

"To bring up a child in the way he should go,
travel that way yourself once in a while."
—JOSH BILLINGS

•

Education is the most powerful weapon which
you can use to change the world.
—NELSON MANDELA

Parents must get across the idea that "I love you always,
but sometimes I do not love your behavior."
—AMY VANDERBILT

Acquire new knowledge whilst thinking over the
old, and you may become a teacher of others.
—CONFUCIUS

Correction does much, but encouragement does more.
Encouragement after censure is as the sun after a shower.
—JOHANN VON GOETHE

Education is what remains after one has forgotten
what one has learned in school.
—**ALBERT EINSTEIN**

The proof that you know something is that you are able to teach it.
—**ARISTOTLE**

"If you want to know the taste of a pear, you must change
the pear by eating it yourself. If you want to know the theory
and methods of revolution, you must take part in revolution.
All genuine knowledge originates in direct experience."
—**MAO TSE-TUNG**

The function of education is to teach one to think
intensively and to think critically. Intelligence plus
character—that is the goal of true education.
—**MARTIN LUTHER KING JR.**

Give a man a fish, and you have fed him for a day.
Teach a man to fish, and you have fed him for the rest of his life.
—**CHINESE PROVERB**

Give a man a fish and he has food for a day;
teach him how to fish and you can get rid
of him for the entire weekend.
—**ANONYMOUS**

Men are born ignorant, not stupid; they are made stupid by education.
—**BERTRAND RUSSELL**

The wise learn many things from their enemies.
—ARISTOPHANES

You are the bows from which your children
as living arrows are sent forth.
—KAHLIL GIBRAN

It's so simple to be wise. Just think of something
stupid to say and then don't say it.
—SAM LEVENSON

"You can tell whether a man is clever by his answers.
You can tell whether a man is wise by his questions."
—NAGUIB MAHFOUZ

Doubt everything at least once,

even the proposition that two times two equals four.

—GEORG C. LICHTENBERG

•

Knowledge is power. Information is liberating.

Education is the premise of progress,

in every society, in every family.

—KOFI ANNAN

•

A foolish consistency is the hobgoblin of little minds.

—RALPH WALDO EMERSON

•

Don't let schooling interfere with your education.

—MARK TWAIN

Nothing is more important for the public welfare than
to form and train our youth in wisdom and virtue.
— BENJAMIN FRANKLIN

Never look down on anyone unless you're helping him up.
— JESSE JACKSON

The only real mistake is the one from which we learn nothing.
— JOHN POWELL

Formal education will make you a living.
Self-education will make you a fortune.
— JIM ROHN

Have a feedback loop, where you're constantly thinking about
what you've done and how you could be doing it better.

—ELON MUSK

•

Learn all you can about people in other parts of the world.
Understanding how people in other countries live and work and
play teaches us to respect them and promotes peace everywhere.

—CAROL BELLAMY

•

Real education should educate us out of self into something far
finer; into a selflessness which links us with all humanity.

—NANCY ASTOR

•

Never doubt that a small group of thoughtful, concerned citizens
can change the world. Indeed it is the only thing that ever has.

—MARGARET MEAD

Leaders think and talk about the solutions.

Followers think and talk about the problems.

—BRIAN TRACY

Around here we don't look backwards for very long. We keep moving

forward, opening up new doors and doing new things, because

we're curious—and curiosity keeps leading us down new paths.

—WALT DISNEY

Learning is not attained by chance, it must be sought

for with ardor and attended to with diligence.

—ABIGAIL ADAMS

Example isn't another way to teach, it is the only way to teach.

—ALBERT EINSTEIN

I've learned that the best classroom in the world
is at the feet of an elderly person.
—ANDY ROONEY

Learning is not a spectator sport.
—ANONYMOUS

Thank goodness I was never sent to school;
it would have rubbed off some of the originality.
—BEATRIX POTTER

If a man empties his purse into his head, no man can take it away
from him. An investment in knowledge always pays the best interest.
—BEN FRANKLIN

Few things help an individual more than to place responsibility upon him and let him know that you trust him.

—BOOKER T. WASHINGTON

One looks back with appreciation to the brilliant teachers, but with gratitude to those who touched our human feelings. The curriculum is so much necessary raw material, but warmth is a vital element for the growing plant and for the soul of the child.

—CARL JUNG

Children want the same things we want. To laugh, to be challenged, to be entertained, and delighted.

—DR. SEUSS [THEODOR GEISEL]

Learning is not compulsory. Neither is survival.

—DR. W. EDWARDS DEMING

I like a teacher who gives you something to take
home to think about besides homework.
—EDITH ANN [LILY TOMLIN]

If the only tool you have is a hammer, you
tend to see every problem as a nail.
—ABRAHAM MASLOW

You can teach a student a lesson for a day; but if you
can teach him to learn by creating curiosity, he will
continue the learning process as long as he lives.
—CLAY P. BEDFORD

A man's mind, stretched by new ideas, may
never return to its original dimensions.
—OLIVER WENDELL HOLMES JR.

Chapter Two

- - - - - - - - -

Quit When the Gorilla Is Tired

{Advice on Life and Living}

[Life] is a little like wrestling a gorilla. You don't quit when
you're tired—you quit when the gorilla is tired.
—ROBERT STRAUSS

You can get much further with a kind word and a
gun than you can with a kind word alone.
—AL CAPONE

Don't hurry. Don't worry. You're only here for a short
visit. So don't forget to stop and smell the roses.
—WALTER HAGEN

Never go to a doctor whose office plants have died.
—ERMA BOMBECK

·

"Saying 'Gesundheit!' doesn't really help the common
cold, but it's every bit as effective as anything
the medical profession has prescribed."
—ANONYMOUS

·

Choose freedom over fear.
—JANELLE MONAE

·

Be careful about reading health books. You may die of a misprint.
—MARK TWAIN

"Yesterday is a canceled check; tomorrow is a promissory note; today is the only cash you have, so spend it wisely."
—KAY LYONS

•

Make it your intention to serve through your life with purpose—you will have a blessed life.
—OPRAH WINFREY

•

Happy the man, and happy he alone, He who can call today his own; He who, secure within, can say, "Tomorrow do thy worst, for I have lived today."
—HORACE,
AS TRANSLATED BY JOHN DRYDEN

Health is the greatest gift, contentment the greatest
wealth, faithfulness the best relationship.
—BUDDHA

We are all in this together.
—HELEN MIRREN

In baiting a mousetrap with cheese,
be sure to leave room for the mouse.
—H. H. MUNRO (SAKI)

Keep cool; anger is not an argument.
—DANIEL WEBSTER

There is one piece of advice, in a life of study, which I
think no one will object to; and that is, every now and
then to be completely idle—to do nothing at all.
—SYDNEY SMITH

"The time to relax is when you don't have time for it."
—SYDNEY J. HARRIS

An important way you can serve and lead is by
helping build resilience in the world.
—SHERYL SANDBERG

The only way to get rid of a temptation is to yield to it.
—OSCAR WILDE

Don't worry about avoiding temptation . . .
as you grow older, it will avoid you.
—WINSTON CHURCHILL

The most important skill you need is asking "What am I not seeing?"
—FAREED ZAKARIA

There's only one corner of the universe you can be
certain of improving, and that's your own self.
—ALDOUS HUXLEY

Have no fear of perfection—you'll never reach it.
—**SALVADOR DALI**

•

"Never lend your car to anyone to whom you have given birth."
—**ERMA BOMBECK**

•

Life is an echo—what you send out comes back.
—**ANONYMOUS**

•

The wise man will always reflect concerning
the quality, not the quantity, of life.
—**LUCIUS ANNAEUS SENECA**

Do not try to live forever. You will not succeed.
—**GEORGE BERNARD SHAW**

•

"If you're going to do something tonight that you'll
be sorry for tomorrow morning, sleep late."
—**HENNY YOUNGMAN**

•

Don't eat yellow snow.
—**ANONYMOUS**

•

Half our life is spent trying to find something to do with
the time we have rushed through life trying to save.
—**WILL ROGERS**

Don't carry a grudge. While you're carrying the
grudge, the other guy's out dancing.
—**BUDDY HACKETT**

Life is change. Growth is optional. Choose wisely.
—**KAREN KAISER CLARK**

When you come to a fork in the road, take it.
—**YOGI BERRA**

Never try to teach a pig to sing.
It wastes your time and annoys the pig.
—**SOURCE UNKNOWN**

When one door closes, another one opens, but we often
look so long and regretfully at the closed door that
we fail to see the one that has opened for us.
—ALEXANDER GRAHAM BELL

"A man has to live with himself, and he should see
to it that he always has good company."
—CHARLES EVANS HUGHES

Retirement kills more people than hard work ever did.
—MALCOLM FORBES

He who has health has hope. And he who has hope has everything.
—ARABIAN PROVERB

He that finds discontentment in one place is
not likely to find happiness in another.
—**AESOP**, *THE ASS AND HIS MASTERS*

Age is not important unless you're a cheese.
—**HELEN HAYES**

What's a man's first duty? The answer's brief: to be himself.
—**HENRIK IBSEN**

What the hell—you might be right, you might
be wrong . . . but don't just avoid.
—**KATHARINE HEPBURN**

You don't stop laughing because you grow older.

You grow older because you stop laughing.

—**MAURICE CHEVALIER**

⬤

The attributes of a great lady may still be found in the rule of

the four S's: Sincerity, Simplicity, Sympathy, and Serenity.

—**EMILY POST**

⬤

It is dangerous to be sincere unless you are also stupid.

—**GEORGE BERNARD SHAW**

⬤

If someone offers you a breath mint, accept it.

—**H. JACKSON BROWN**

The whole business of marshaling one's energies becomes
more and more important as one grows older.
—HUME CRONYN

"In matters of grave importance, style,
not sincerity, is the vital thing."
—OSCAR WILDE

Love yourself, respect yourself. Never sell yourself short. Believe
in yourself regardless of what people think. You can accomplish
anything, absolutely anything, if you set your mind to it.
—MARCUS ALLEN

A good time for laughing is when you can.
—JESSAMYN WEST

Do not take life too seriously. You will
never get out of it alive.
—**ELBERT HUBBARD**

Do not go gentle into that good night but rage,
rage against the dying of the light.
—**DYLAN THOMAS**

"Subdue your appetites,
my dears, and you've
conquered human nature."
—**DOROTHY CANFIELD FISHER**

A man should never be ashamed to admit he has been
in the wrong, which is but saying, in other words,
that he is wiser today than he was yesterday.
—ALEXANDER POPE

As I grow older, I pay less attention to what
men say. I just watch what they do.
—ANDREW CARNEGIE

In the fight between you and the world, back the world.
—FRANZ KAFKA

Expecting the world to treat you fairly because you are good is like
expecting the bull not to charge because you are a vegetarian.
—DENNIS WHOLEY

Always acknowledge a fault frankly. This will throw those in
authority off their guard and give you opportunity to commit more.
—MARK TWAIN

Nothing is more responsible for the good old days than a bad memory.
—FRANKLIN P. ADAMS

If you're going to kick authority in the teeth,
you might as well use two feet.
—KEITH RICHARDS

Always do sober what you said you'd do drunk. That
will teach you to keep your mouth shut.
—ERNEST HEMINGWAY

Age appears to be best in four things; old wood best to burn, old
wine to drink, old friends to trust, and old authors to read.
—SIR FRANCIS BACON

Don't worry about the world coming to an end
today. It's already tomorrow in Australia.
—CHARLES SCHULZ

"The etiquette advice you need is how to say no politely.
You do it cheerfully, with apologies but no excuses. 'I'm so sorry,
I can't this time; I hope you find someone' is all that is necessary."
—JUDITH MARTIN (MISS MANNERS)

Youth is the gift of nature, but age is a work of art.
—STANISLAW JERZY LEC

It is not what we do, but also what we
do not do, for which we are accountable.
—JEAN-BAPTISTE MOLIÈRE

"Teach thy tongue to say 'I do not know,' and thou shalt progress."
—MOSES MAIMONIDES

Here is my biggest takeaway after 60 years on the planet:
There is great value in being fearless. For too much of my life,
I was too afraid, too frightened by it all.
That fear is one of my biggest regrets.
—DIANE KEATON

Knowing is not enough; we must apply.

Willing is not enough; we must do.

—JOHANN VON GOETHE

You never know what is enough unless you

know what is more than enough.

—WILLIAM BLAKE

A clear conscience is usually the sign of a bad memory.

—STEPHEN WRIGHT

It takes courage to grow up and become who you really are.

—E E CUMMINGS

From what we get, we can make a living;

what we give, however, makes a life.

—ARTHUR ASHE

Start by doing what is necessary; then do what is possible;

and suddenly you are doing the impossible.

—ST. FRANCIS OF ASSISI

You can't do anything about the length of your life, but

you can do something about its width and depth.

—H. L. MENCKEN

By the time a man is wise enough to watch his

step, he's too old to go anywhere.

—BILLY CRYSTAL

Life should not be a journey to the grave with the intention of arriving safely in a pretty and well preserved body, but rather to skid in broadside in a cloud of smoke, thoroughly used up, totally worn out, and loudly proclaiming "Wow! What a Ride!"

—HUNTER S. THOMPSON

"A young man who desires to know all that in all ages in all lands has been thought by the best minds, and wishes to make a synthesis of all these thoughts for the future benefit of mankind, is laying up for himself a very miserable old age."

—MAX BEERBOHM

Don't go around saying the world owes you a living. The world owes you nothing. It was here first.

—MARK TWAIN

When a person doesn't have gratitude, something is missing in his or her humanity. A person can almost be defined by his or her attitude toward gratitude.

—**ELIE WIESEL**

I was training to be an electrician. I suppose I got wired the wrong way round somewhere along the line.

—**ELVIS PRESLEY**

You gain strength, courage, and confidence by every experience in which you really stop to look fear in the face. You are able to say to yourself, "I lived through this horror. I can take the next thing that comes along."

—**ELEANOR ROOSEVELT**

You've got to be very careful if you don't know where
you are going, because you might not get there.
—**YOGI BERRA**

Nature gives you the face you have at twenty; it is
up to you to merit the face you have at fifty.
—**COCO CHANEL**

Why is it that we rejoice at a wedding and cry at a funeral?
It is because we are not the person involved.
—**MARK TWAIN**

Neither should a ship rely on one small anchor,
nor should life rest on a single hope.
—**EPICTETUS**

Success is just a war of attrition. Sure, there's an element of talent you should probably possess. But if you just stick around long enough, eventually something is going to happen.
—DAX SHEPARD

When people talk, listen completely. Most people never listen.
—ERNEST HEMINGWAY

A day without laughter is a day wasted.
—CHARLIE CHAPLIN

"Be thankful for what you have; you'll end up having more. If you concentrate on what you don't have, you will never, ever have enough."
—OPRAH WINFREY

You must try to generate happiness within yourself.
If you aren't happy in one place,
chances are you won't be happy anyplace.
—ERNIE BANKS

Man, I really like Vegas.
—ELVIS PRESLEY

The true measure of an individual is how he treats a
person who can do him absolutely no good.
—ANN LANDERS

Motivation is a fire from within. If someone else tries to light
that fire under you, chances are it will burn very briefly.
—STEPHEN R. COVEY

You can have anything you want if you are willing
to give up the belief that you can't have it.
—**ROBERT ANTHONY**

A true friend is one who overlooks your
failures and tolerates your success!
—**DOUG LARSON**

It's a funny thing about life: If you refuse to accept
anything but the very best, you will very often get it.
—**W. SOMERSET MAUGHAM**

You have to find it. No one else can find it for you.
—**BJORN BORG**

Memory is a marvelous thing—it enables you to
remember a mistake each time you repeat it.
—MAX KAUFMAN

"Remember, no one can make you feel inferior without your consent."
—ELEANOR ROOSEVELT

If thine enemy offend thee, give his child a drum.
—CHINESE CURSE

Always forgive your enemies; nothing annoys them so much.
—OSCAR WILDE

When the water reaches the upper level, follow the rats.
—CLAUDE SWANSON

It is better to die on your feet than to live on your knees.
—EMILIANO ZAPATA

"Death is not the greatest loss in life.
The greatest loss is what dies inside us while we live."
—NORMAN COUSINS

Dying is a very dull, dreary affair.
And my advice to you is to have nothing whatever to do with it.
—W. SOMERSET MAUGHAM

That you may retain your self-respect, it is better to displease
the people by doing what you know is right, than to
temporarily please them by doing what you know is wrong.
—WILLIAM J. H. BOETCKER

It is amazing what you can accomplish if you
do not care who gets the credit.
—HARRY S. TRUMAN

The only people with whom you should try to get
even are those who have helped you.
—JOHN E. SOUTHARD

If we listened to our intellect, we'd never have a love affair. We'd never have a friendship. We'd never go into business, because we'd be too cynical. Well, that's nonsense. You've got to jump off the cliffs all the time and build your wings on the way down.
—ANNIE DILLARD

I must respect the opinions of others even if I disagree with them.
—HERBERT H. LEHMAN

"Good character is contagious; pass it on to others."
—ANONYMOUS

It's lack of faith that makes people afraid of meeting challenges, and I believed in myself.
—MUHAMMAD ALI

"Play the hand you're dealt."
—ANONYMOUS

"Don't look back. Something might be gaining on you."
—SATCHEL PAIGE

The "uh-oh" moments are worth cherishing just as much as "ah-ha" moments: Mistakes, failures, embarrassments and disappointments are a necessary component of growing wise. We can learn more from our not-so-good experiences than we can learn from our good ones.
—SONIA SOTOMAYOR

There is a need for audacious hope.
—CORNELL WEST

If you do not tell the truth about yourself you
cannot tell it about other people.

—VIRGINIA WOOLF

Don't waste your time thinking about who you ought
to be; just be content with who you're becoming.

—ANONYMOUS

Be pleasant until ten o'clock in the morning and
the rest of the day will take care of itself.

—ELBERT HUBBARD

At the end of your days, you will be judged by

your gallop, not by your stumble.

—BRADLEY WHITFORD

Say yes.

—STEPHEN COLBERT

Failure can be awful. But living so cautiously

that you never fail is worse.

—J. K. ROWLING

Think in the morning. Act in the noon.

Eat in the evening. Sleep in the night.

—WILLIAM BLAKE

Always go to other people's funerals,

otherwise they won't come to yours.

—YOGI BERRA

"The first recipe for happiness is:

Avoid too lengthy meditation on the past."

—ANDRÉ MAUROIS

You can only milk a cow so long,

and then you're left holding the pail.

—HANK AARON

It does no good to think moralistically about how much

time we waste. Wasted time is usually good soul time.

—THOMAS MOORE

Never let your sense of morals get in the way of doing what's right.

—ISAAC ASIMOV

"Nothing ruins the truth like stretching it."

—ANONYMOUS

Flattery won't hurt you if you don't swallow it.

—KIN (FRANK MCKINNEY) HUBBARD

"If you have enough butter, anything is good."

—JULIA CHILD

"Life is uncertain. Eat dessert first."
— E R N E S T I N E   U L M E R

•

One of these days in your travels, a guy is going to come up to you
and show you a nice brand-new deck of cards on which the seal
is not yet broken, and this guy is going to offer to bet you that he
can make the Jack of Spades jump out of the deck and squirt cider
in your ear. But, son, do not bet this man, for as sure as you are
standing there, you are going to end up with an earful of cider.
— D A M O N   R U N Y O N

•

You can be as earnest and ridiculous as you need
to be, if you don't attempt it in isolation.
— B A R B A R A   K I N G S O L V E R

Don't muck up the world worse than it already is.
—RUSSELL BAKER

•

If you're offered a seat on a rocket ship, don't ask what seat. Just get on.
—SHERYL SANDBERG

•

Dress simply. If you wear a dinner jacket, don't wear
anything else on it . . . like lunch or dinner.
—GEORGE BURNS

•

Start every day off with a smile and get it over with.
—W. C. FIELDS

"You've got to take the bitter with the sour."
—SAMUEL GOLDWYN

Never purchase beauty products in a hardware store.
—MISS PIGGY

"The secret to staying young is to live honestly,

eat slowly, and lie about your age."
—LUCILLE BALL

The greatest thing in the world is to know how to belong to oneself.
—MICHEL DE MONTAIGNE

Age is whatever you think it is.
You are as old as you think you are.
—MUHAMMAD ALI

•

Stewart [Brand] and his team put out several issues of the *Whole Earth Catalog*, and then when it had run its course, they put out a final issue. . . . On the back cover of their final issue was a photograph of an early morning country road, the kind you might find yourself hitchhiking on if you were so adventurous. Beneath were the words, "Stay hungry, stay foolish." It was their farewell message as they signed off. "Stay hungry, stay foolish."
—STEVE JOBS

•

If you're going to be able to look back on something and laugh about it, you might as well laugh about it now.
—MARIE OSMOND

Live your life like it's your second chance.

—SALMAN KHAN

Do the stuff that only you can do.

—NEIL GAIMAN

Everything you are comes from your choices.

—JEFF BEZOS

Success is a lot like a bright white tuxedo. You feel terrific when you get it, but then you're desperately afraid of getting it dirty, of spoiling it.

—CONAN O'BRIEN

"There are two things to aim for in life: first, to get when you want; and, after that, to enjoy it. Only the wisest of mankind achieve the second."
—LOGAN PEARSALL SMITH

Life is an adventure in forgiveness.
—NORMAN COUSINS

Do whatever comes your way to do as well as you can. Think as little as possible about yourself. Think as much as possible about other people. Dwell on things that are interesting. Since you get more joy out of giving joy to others, you should put a good deal of thought into the happiness that you are able to give.
—ELEANOR ROOSEVELT

Anyone who has never made a mistake has never tried anything new.
—ALBERT EINSTEIN

It is better to ask some of the questions than to know all the answers.
—JAMES THURBER

You must live for what you believe in and believe in what you live for.
—ANONYMOUS

When you see something that is not right, not fair,

not just, you must have the courage to stand up,

to speak up, and find a way to get in the way.
—JOHN LEWIS

"You have to trust in something—your gut,
destiny, life, karma, whatever."
—STEVE JOBS

I wish I didn't know now what I didn't know then.
—BOB SEGER

I'm a millionaire, I'm a multi-millionaire. I'm filthy rich. You know
why I'm a multi-millionaire? Cause multi-millions like what I do.
—MICHAEL MOORE

The easiest person to deceive is one's own self.
—EDWARD BULWER-LYTTON

"The unvarnished truth is always better than the best-dressed lie."
—ANN LANDERS

If there was nothing wrong in the world,

there wouldn't be anything for us to do.
—GEORGE BERNARD SHAW

The strongest possible piece of advice I would give to any

young woman is: Don't screw around, and don't smoke.
—EDWINA CURRIE

If a dog will not come to you after having

looked you in the face, you should go home

and examine your conscience.
—WOODROW WILSON

All human beings should try to learn before they die

what they are running from, and to, and why.

—JAMES THURBER

Life is not fair—get used to it!

—BILL GATES

If you really want to do something, you'll find a

way. If you don't, you'll find an excuse.

—JIM ROHN

Rest is not idleness, and to lie sometimes on the grass
under the trees on a summer's day, listening to the
murmur of water, or watching the clouds float across
the blue sky, is by no means a waste of time.

—JOHN LUBBOCK

I came to the conclusion long ago that all life is six to five against.

—DAMON RUNYON

This above all: to thine own self be true,
And it must follow, as the night the day,
Thou canst not then be false to any man.

—POLONIUS, FROM *HAMLET*,
WILLIAM SHAKESPEARE

There must be quite a few things that a hot bath
won't cure, but I don't know many of them.
—SYLVIA PLATH

You are only young once, but you can stay immature indefinitely.
—OGDEN NASH

Retirement is the ugliest word in the language.
—ERNEST HEMINGWAY

Be *happy* with what you have. Be *excited* about what you want.
—ALAN COHEN

We forge the chains we wear in life.
— CHARLES DICKENS

Life is a journey, and if you fall in love with the
journey, you will be in love forever.
— PETER HAGERTY

For me it is sufficient to have a corner by my hearth, a book,
and a friend, and a nap undisturbed by creditors or grief.
— FERNANDEZ DE ANDRADA

The art of living lies less in eliminating our
troubles than growing with them.
— BERNARD M. BARUCH

We all get report cards in many different ways, but the real
excitement of what you're doing is in the doing of it. It's not
what you're going get in the end—it's not the final curtain—
it's really in the doing it, and loving what you're doing.
—RALPH LAUREN

Anxiety is the dizziness of freedom.
—SOREN KIERKEGAARD

View your life from your funeral, looking back at your life experiences,
what have you accomplished? What would you have wanted to
accomplish but didn't? What were the happy moments?
What were the sad? What would you do again, and what you wouldn't?
—VICTOR FRANKL

Use a travel delay as opportunity to stop rather than
get stressed. When the world stands still, let it.
—KARL DURRANT

Mostly nothing is that serious as it seems in the first moment.
—JULIAN POLLMAN

My two favourite things in life are libraries and bicycles.
They both move people forward without wasting anything.
The perfect day: riding a bike to the library.
—PETER GOLKIN

Find your focus by seeking all that is good in your life.
—LORII MYERS

We got life to live, not to survive, do the things you
always want to and be the person you always desire
to be. Don't let other people deal with it.
—RIDHDHESH JIVAWALA

A good life is a collection of happy moments.
—DENIS WAITLEY

Live to give and be rich of heart and laughter.
—AMY LEIGH MERCREE

It's easier to maintain a good character than
to recover it when it's gone bad.
—ISRAELMORE AYIVOR

A man who dares to waste one hour of time
has not discovered the value of life.
—CHARLES DARWIN

Life is not about how fast you run or how high
you climb, but how well you bounce.
—VIVIAN KOMORI

We are always getting ready to live but never living.
— RALPH WALDO EMERSON

I can get sad, I can get frustrated, I can get scared, but I
never get depressed because there's joy in my life.
—MICHAEL J. FOX

The first step to getting the things you want out
of life is this: Decide what you want.
—BEN STEIN

Not a shred of evidence exists in favor of the idea that life is serious.
— BRENDAN GILL

A man's life is interesting primarily when he has failed—
I well know. For it's a sign that he tried to surpass himself.
— GEORGES CLEMENCEAU

Maxim for life: You get treated in life the
way you teach people to treat you.
— WAYNE DYER

The most important thing in life is not the triumph but the struggle.
The essential thing is not to have conquered but to have fought well.
— PIERRE DE COUBERTIN

The aim of life is to live, and to live means to be aware,

joyously, drunkenly, serenely, divinely aware.

—HENRY MILLER

Never be bullied into silence. Never allow yourself to be made a

victim. Accept no one's definition of your life, but define yourself.

—HARVEY S. FIRESTONE

Life is what we make it, always has been, always will be.

—GRANDMA MOSES

You need to find a way to live your life, that it

doesn't make a mockery of your values.

—BILL AYERS

Life is a great big canvas, and you should

throw all the paint on it you can.

—DANNY KAYE

I think everybody should get rich and famous and do everything

they ever dreamed of so they can see that it's not the answer.

—JIM CARREY

Life is the game that must be played.

—EDWIN ARLINGTON ROBINSON

Chapter Three

■ ■ ■ ■ ■ ■ ■ ■

Anvil or Hammer

{Advice on Work and Leadership}

Leadership is unlocking people's potential to become better.
— BILL BRADLEY

Victory is sweetest when you've known defeat.
— VICTOR FORBES

In this world a man must either be anvil or hammer.
— HENRY WADSWORTH LONGFELLOW

"The beginning is the most important part of the work."
— PLATO

No labor, however humble, is dishonoring.

—**THE TALMUD**

Every time you have to speak, you are auditioning for leadership.

—**JAMES HUMES**

Be a yardstick of quality. Some people aren't used to
an environment where excellence is expected.

—**STEVE JOBS**

Whether you think you can or you think you can't, you're right.
—**HENRY FORD**

The secret of joy in work is contained in one word: excellence.
To know how to do something well is to enjoy it.
—**PEARL BUCK**

I alone cannot change the world, but I can cast a
stone across the water to create many ripples.
—**MOTHER TERESA**

"The secret of getting ahead is getting started. The secret of getting started is breaking your complex overwhelming tasks into small manageable tasks, and then starting on the first one."
—MARK TWAIN

To kill time is not murder, it's suicide.
—WILLIAM JAMES

The less one has to do, the less time one finds to do it in.
—LORD CHESTERFIELD

"Vision without action is a daydream.
Action without vision is a nightmare."
—JAPANESE PROVERB

"Only one man in a thousand is a leader of
men—the other 999 follow women."
—GROUCHO MARX

Life is 10 percent what happens to me
and 90 percent of how I react to it.
—CHARLES SWINDOLL

If you are planning for one year, grow rice. If you are planning for twenty years, grow trees. If you are planning for centuries, grow men.
—CHINESE PROVERB

"You don't manage people, you manage things. You lead people."
—GRACE HOPPER

A leader is one who sees more than others see, who sees farther than others see, and who sees before others see.
—LEROY EIMES

Give me a stock clerk with a goal and I'll give you a man who will make history. Give me a man with no goals and I'll give you a stock clerk.
—J. C. PENNEY

Expect problems and eat them for breakfast.
—**ALFRED A. MONTAPERT**

●

A genuine leader is not a searcher for consensus

but a molder of consensus.
—**MARTIN LUTHER KING JR.**

●

Control your own destiny or someone else will.
—**JACK WELCH**

●

"Creating without claiming,

Doing without taking credit,

Guiding without interfering,

This is Primal Virtue."
—**LAO-TZU**

We can't solve problems by using the same kind of
thinking we used when we created them.
—ALBERT EINSTEIN

You can't turn back the clock.
But you can wind it up again.
—BONNIE PRUDDEN

Know each other as if you were brothers; negotiate
deals as if you were strangers to each other.
—ARABIAN PROVERB

To handle yourself, use your head; to handle others, use your heart.
—ELEANOR ROOSEVELT

Pull the string, and it will follow wherever you
wish. Push it, and it will go nowhere at all.
—DWIGHT D. EISENHOWER

If you can't convince them, confuse them.
—HARRY S. TRUMAN

"Don't get mad. Don't get even. Just get elected, then get even."
—JAMES CARVILLE

Everything you've ever wanted is on the other side of fear.
—GEORGE ADDAIR

If you do what you've always done, you'll

get what you've always gotten.

—ANTHONY ROBBINS

•

"No one ever won a chess game by betting on each move.

Sometimes you have to move backward to get a step forward."

—AMAR GOPAL BOSE

•

Take rest; a field that has rested gives a bountiful crop.

—OVID

•

Measure twice, cut once.

—CRAFTSMAN'S ADAGE

All of the great leaders have had one characteristic in
common: it was the willingness to confront unequivocally
the major anxiety of their people in their time. This,
and not much else, is the essence of leadership.
—JOHN KENNETH GALBRAITH

A good plan violently executed now is better
than a perfect plan executed next week.
—GEORGE S. PATTON

"Forgive your enemies, but never forget their names."
—JOHN F. KENNEDY

Don't ever take a fence down until you know why it was put up.
—ROBERT FROST

Don't agonize. Organize.

—**FLORYNCE KENNEDY**

•

Stop stewing and start doing!

—**DENIS WAITLEY**

•

Build your own dreams, or someone else will hire you to build theirs.

—**FARRAH GRAY**

•

Work as if you were to live a hundred years.

Pray as if you were to die tomorrow.

—**BENJAMIN FRANKLIN**

I am not discouraged, because every wrong attempt
discarded is another step forward.
—THOMAS A. EDISON

"When I go fishing, I don't bait the hook with something I like to eat."
—WILL ROGERS

You don't lead by hitting people over the head—
that's assault, not leadership.
—DWIGHT D. EISENHOWER

"No one can give you authority. But if you act like
you have it, others will believe you do."
—KAREN IRELAND

There are no office hours for leaders.
—**JAMES CARDINAL GIBBONS**

"Change before you have to."
—**JACK WELCH**

"The way to do research is to attack the facts at
the point of greatest astonishment."
—**CELIA GREEN**

If two men on the same job agree all the time, then one is
unnecessary. If they disagree all the time, then both are useless.
—**DARRYL ZANUCK**

Presence is more than just being there.
—MALCOLM FORBES

Â·

The best way to escape from a problem is to solve it.
—ALAN SAPORTA

Â·

You are your work. Don't trade the stuff of your life, time,
for nothing more than dollars. That's a rotten bargain.
—RITA MAE BROWN

Â·

You can either take action, or you can hang back and hope for
a miracle. Miracles are great, but they are so unpredictable.
—PETER F. DRUCKER

"When a thing is done, it's done. Don't look back.

Look forward to your next objective."

—GEORGE C. MARSHALL

The secret of business is to know something nobody else knows.

—ARISTOTLE ONASSIS

I once complained to my father that I didn't seem to be able to do things the same way other people did. Dad's advice? "Margo, don't be a sheep. People hate sheep. They eat sheep."

—MARGO KAUFMAN

"The best executive is the one who has sense enough to pick good men to do what he wants done, and self restraint enough to keep from meddling with them while they do it."

—THEODORE ROOSEVELT

"A constructive, useful life, good works, and good relationships
are as valid as writing poetry or inventing a machine. Anything
that one does well and obtains satisfaction from is a good
enough reason for living. To be a decent human being that
people like and feel better for knowing is enough."
—ROBERT GOULD

Great leaders are almost always great simplifiers,
who can cut through argument, debate, and doubt
to offer a solution everybody can understand.
—COLIN POWELL

Victory has a hundred fathers and defeat is an orphan.
—JOHN F. KENNEDY

Never ascribe to malice that which can adequately
be explained by incompetence.
—NAPOLEON BONAPARTE

You have to learn to treat people as a resource. . . .

You have to ask not what do they cost, but what

is the yield, what can they produce?

— PETER F. DRUCKER

A leader is not an administrator who loves to run others,

but someone who carries water for his people so

that they can get on with their jobs.

— ROBERT TOWNSEND

In matters of style, swim with the current;

in matters of principle, stand like a rock.

— THOMAS JEFFERSON

If you hear a voice within you say, "You cannot paint,"

then by all means paint and that voice will be silenced.

— VINCENT VAN GOGH

Be nice to people on your way up because
you'll meet them on your way down.
—**WILSON MIZNER**

Big doesn't necessarily mean better.
Sunflowers aren't better than violets.
—**EDNA FERBER**

Often you just have to rely on your intuition.
—**BILL GATES**

"Security isn't what the wise person looks for; it's opportunity."
—**EARL NIGHTINGALE**

There are two ways of spreading light: to be the
candle or the mirror that reflects it.
—EDITH WHARTON

There are three essentials to leadership: humility, clarity and courage.
—FUCHAN YUAN

To have long term success as a coach or in any position
of leadership, you have to be obsessed in some way.
—PAT RILEY

Keep your fears to yourself, but share your courage with others.
—ROBERT LOUIS STEVENSON

It's not so much how busy you are, but why you are busy.

The bee is praised. The mosquito is swatted.

—**MARY O'CONNOR**

•

"Everyone is a genius at least once a year;

a real genius has his original ideas closer together."

—**GEORG C. LICHTENBERG**

•

Take your work seriously, but never yourself.

—**MARGOT FONTEYN**

•

Don't look at the problem. The more you look at problems,

the more problems will come. Look for the solution.

—**LISA PRAGNELLE**

You have to learn the rules of the game—
and then you have to play better than anyone else.
— DIANNE FEINSTEIN

Management is about arranging and telling.
Leadership is about nurturing and enhancing.
— TOM PETERS

No man will make a great leader who wants to do it
all himself, or to get all the credit for doing it.
— ANDREW CARNEGIE

One of the tests of leadership is the ability to recognize
a problem before it becomes an emergency.
— ARNOLD GLASOW

"Being responsible sometimes means pissing people off."
—COLIN POWELL

•

Those who say it can't be done are usually
interrupted by others doing it.
—JAMES A. BALDWIN

•

To fulfill a dream, to be allowed to sweat over lonely
labor, to be given a chance to create, is the meat
and potatoes of life. The money is the gravy.
—BETTE DAVIS

•

The role of leadership is to transform the complex
situation into small pieces and prioritize them.
—CARLOS GHOSN

A leader is a dealer in hope.
— **NAPOLEON BONAPARTE**

Management is doing things right;
leadership is doing the right things.
— **PETER F. DRUCKER**

Enlightened leadership is spiritual if we understand spirituality
not as some kind of religious dogma or ideology but as
the domain of awareness where we experience values like
truth, goodness, beauty, love and compassion, and also
intuition, creativity, insight and focused attention.
— **DEEPAK CHOPRA**

If you don't have time to do it right, you must have time to do it over.
— **ANONYMOUS**

Take calculated risks. That is quite different from being rash.
— GEORGE S. PATTON

•

"Get action. Do things; be sane, don't fritter away your time; create,
act, take a place wherever you are and be somebody; get action.
Seize the moment. Man was never intended to become an oyster."
— THEODORE ROOSEVELT

•

Quigley's Law: Whoever has any authority over you,
no matter how small, will attempt to use it.
— ANONYMOUS

•

"If you wish to know what a man is, place him in authority."
— YUGOSLAV PROVERB

No pressure, no diamonds.

—MARY CASE

•

Do not confuse motion and progress. A rocking horse
keeps moving but does not make any progress.

—ALFRED A. MONTAPERT

•

Average leaders raise the bar on themselves; good leaders raise the
bar for others; great leaders inspire others to raise their own bar.

—ORRIN WOODWARD

•

He who has never learned to obey cannot be a good commander.

—ARISTOTLE

Problems are only opportunities in work clothes.
—HENRY J. KAISER

Leadership is not about a title or a designation. It's about impact,
influence and inspiration. Impact involves getting results,
influence is about spreading the passion you have for your
work, and you have to inspire team-mates and customers.
—ROBIN S. SHARMA

A leader is one who knows the way, goes the way, and shows the way.
—JOHN C. MAXWELL

Life without industry is guilt, and industry without art is brutality.
—JOHN RUSKIN

You can't build a reputation on what you intend to do.
—LIZ SMITH

Work smarter, not harder—
laziness is the mother of invention.
—REGINA REYNOLDS

"You never get a second chance to make a first impression."
—ANONYMOUS

In short, the way to wealth, if you desire it, is as plain as the way to market. It depends chiefly on two words, industry and frugality; that is, waste neither time nor money, but make the best use of both.
—BENJAMIN FRANKLIN

The secret of getting ahead is getting started.
—SALLY BERGER

•

I am not afraid of an army of lions led by a sheep;
I am afraid of an army of sheep led by a lion.
—ALEXANDER THE GREAT

•

Only the guy who isn't rowing has time to rock the boat.
—JEAN-PAUL SARTRE

•

A ruler should be slow to punish and swift to reward.
—OVID

The function of leadership is to produce
more leaders, not more followers.
—RALPH NADER

Don't worry about people stealing your ideas. If your ideas are
any good, you'll have to ram them down people's throats.
—HOWARD AIKEN

Excellence in any department can be attained only by the
labor of a lifetime; it is not to be purchased at a lesser price.
—SAMUEL JOHNSON

If you want creative workers, give them enough time to play.

—JOHN CLEESE

If you break 100, watch your golf.

If you break 80, watch your business.

—JOEY ADAMS

Everyone has an invisible sign hanging from their
neck saying, "Make me feel important." Never forget
this message when working with people.

—MARY KAY ASH

"Never say no when a client asks for something, even if it is the moon. You can always try, and anyhow, there is plenty of time afterwards to explain that it was not possible."
—RICHARD M. NIXON

It's all to do with the training.
You can do a lot if you're properly trained.
—QUEEN ELIZABETH II

Education is the mother of leadership.
—WENDELL WILLKIE

I look for what needs to be done. After all,

that's how the universe designs itself.

—R. BUCKMINSTER FULLER

I have always supported measures and principles and not men.

—DAVY CROCKETT

"My grandfather once told me that there were two kinds of people:
those who do the work and those who take the credit. He told me
to try to be in the first group. There was much less competition."

—INDIRA GANDHI

Every time you have to speak, you are auditioning for leadership.

—JAMES HUMES

You are not here merely to make a living. You are here in order to enable the world to live more amply, with greater vision, with a finer spirit of hope and achievement. You are here to enrich the world, and you impoverish yourself if you forget the errand.

—WOODROW WILSON

I can give you a six-word formula for success:
Think things through—then follow through.

—EDDIE RICKENBACKER

One of the tests of leadership is the ability to recognize a problem before it becomes an emergency.

—ARNOLD GLASOW

Becoming a leader is synonymous with becoming yourself.
It is precisely that simple and it is also that difficult.

—WARREN BENNIS

Wisdom is knowing what to do next, skill is
knowing how to do it, and virtue is doing it.
—DAVID STAR JORDAN

Control is not leadership; management is not leadership; leadership
is leadership. If you seek to lead, invest at least 50 percent of your
time in leading yourself—your own purpose, ethics, principles,
motivation, conduct. Invest at least 20 percent leading those
with authority over you and 15 percent leading your peers.
—DEE HOCK

Leaders don't inflict pain, they share pain.
—MAX DEPREE

The art of leadership is saying no, not saying
yes. It is very easy to say yes.
—TONY BLAIR

The highest of distinctions is service to others.

—KING GEORGE VI

If you're not sure where you are going, you're

liable to end up someplace else.

—ROBERT F. MAGER

Anyone can hold the helm when the sea is calm.

—PUBLILIUS SYRUS

Become the kind of leader that people would follow

voluntarily, even if you had no title or position.

—BRIAN TRACY

A leader is not an administrator who loves to run others, but someone
who carries water for his people so that they can get on with their jobs.
—ROBERT TOWNSEND

Leadership cannot really be taught. It can only be learned.
—HAROLD GENEEN

Look over your shoulder now and then to
be sure someone's following you.
—HENRY GILMER

You cannot be a leader, and ask other people to follow
you, unless you know how to follow, too.
—SAM RAYBURN

It's hard to lead a cavalry charge if you think you look funny on a horse.
— ADLAI E. STEVENSON II

A leader is a dealer in hope.
— NAPOLEON BONAPARTE

The leaders who offer blood, toil, tears and sweat always get more out of their followers than those who offer safety and a good time. When it comes to the pinch, human beings are heroic.
— GEORGE ORWELL

A leader takes people where they want to go. A great leader takes people where they don't necessarily want to go, but ought to be.
— ROSALYNN CARTER

A leader is best when people barely know he exists, when his work is done, his aim fulfilled, they will say: we did it ourselves.
—LAO TZU

If your actions inspire others to dream more, learn more, do more and become more, you are a leader.
—JOHN QUINCY ADAMS

A leader is like a shepherd. He stays behind the flock, letting the most nimble go out ahead, whereupon the others follow, not realizing that all along they are being directed from behind.
—NELSON MANDELA

He who has never learned to obey cannot be a good commander.
—ARISTOTLE

Earn your leadership every day.
— MICHAEL JORDAN

Leadership is lifting a person's vision to high sights, the
raising of a person's performance to a higher standard, the
building of a personality beyond its normal limitations.
— PETER DRUCKER

If you think you are leading and turn around to see no
one following, then you are just taking a walk.
— BENJAMIN HOOKS

A man who wants to lead the orchestra

must turn his back on the crowd.

—MAX LUCADO

A cowardly leader is the most dangerous of men.

—STEVEN KING

Outstanding leaders go out of their way to boost the

self-esteem of their personnel. If people believe in

themselves, it's amazing what they can accomplish.

—SAM WALTON

Chapter Four

■ ■ ■ ■ ■ ■ ■ ■

Love What You Are Doing

{Advice on Success—and the Money
that Sometimes Comes with It}

Anyone can be a millionaire, but to become a billionaire you need an astrologer. Keep your eyes on the stars, learn from the best.

—JOHN PIERPONT MORGAN

Rule No.1: Never lose money. Rule No.2: Never forget rule No.1.

—WARREN BUFFETT

Success is not the key to happiness.

Happiness is the key to success.

If you love what you are doing, you will be successful.

—ALBERT SCHWEITZER

Love what you do. Get good at it. Competence is a rare commodity in this day and age. And let the chips fall where they may.

— JON STEWART

You can have it all. You just can't have it all at one time.

— OPRAH WINFREY

Financial independence is paramount. My mom always says that when a woman is financially independent, she has the ability to live life on her own terms. I think that was the soundest advice that I ever got. No matter where you go in life or who you get married to, you have to be financially independent—whether you use it or not.

— PRIYANKA CHOPRA

Do not be embarrassed by your failures,

learn from them and start again.

—RICHARD BRANSON

"A true measure of your worth includes all the benefits

others have gained from your success."

—CULLEN HIGHTOWER

A strong, positive self-image is the best possible preparation for success.

—DR. JOYCE BROTHERS

Keep away from people who try to belittle your ambitions.
Small people always do that, but the really great make
you feel that you, too, can become great.

—MARK TWAIN

Instead of thinking about where you are, think
about where you want to be. It takes twenty years of
hard work to become an overnight success.

—DIANA RANKIN

Money and success don't change people;
they merely amplify what is already there.

—WILL SMITH

Failure isn't fatal, but failure to change might be.
—JOHN WOODEN

Everything you want is on the other side of fear.
—JACK CANFIELD

"If one advances confidently in the direction of one's dreams,
and endeavors to live the life which one has imagined, one
will meet with a success unexpected in common hours."
—HENRY DAVID THOREAU

Try not to become a person of success, but
rather try to become a person of value.
—ALBERT EINSTEIN

It is not the strongest of the species that survive, nor the
most intelligent, but the one most responsive to change.
—CHARLES DARWIN

Great minds discuss ideas; average minds discuss
events; small minds discuss people.
—ELEANOR ROOSEVELT

Don't aim for success if you want it; just do what you
love and believe in, and it will come naturally.
— DAVID FROST

Look at the real successes, the people who make a lot more
money than you—Elton John, Captain Kangaroo, anybody
from Saudi Arabia, Big Bird, and so on. They all dress
funny—and they all succeed. Are you catching on?
— DAVE BARRY

Part of the secret of a success in life is to eat what
you like and let the food fight it out inside.
— MARK TWAIN

Formula for success: Underpromise and overdeliver.
— TOM PETERS

Only those who dare to fail greatly can ever achieve greatly.
—ROBERT F. KENNEDY

There are no secrets to success. It is the result of
preparation, hard work, and learning from failure.
—COLIN POWELL

I can accept failure, everyone fails at something.
But I can't accept not trying.
—MICHAEL JORDAN

"The test of a successful person is not an ability to eliminate all problems before they arise, but to meet and work out difficulties when they do arise. We must be willing to make an intelligent compromise with perfection lest we wait forever before taking action. It's still good advice to cross bridges as we come to them."
—DAVID JOSEPH SCHWARTZ

Successful leaders make sure that they succeed! They are not afraid of strength in others. Andrew Carnegie wanted to put on his gravestone, "Here lies a man who knew how to put into his service more able men than he was himself."
—PETER F. DRUCKER

The successful warrior is the average man, with laser-like focus.
—BRUCE LEE

Keep on going, and the chances are that you will stumble on something, perhaps when you are least expecting it. I never heard of anyone ever stumbling on something sitting down.
— CHARLES F. KETTERING

In my experience, there is only one motivation, and that is desire. No reasons or principle contain it or stand against it.
— JANE SMILEY

Success does not consist in never making mistakes but in never making the same one a second time.
— GEORGE BERNARD SHAW

My tombstone? I'm thinking something along the lines of, "Geez, he was just here a minute ago."
— GEORGE CARLIN

"If you are willing to do more than you are paid to do,
eventually you will be paid to do more than you do."
—ANONYMOUS

•

If you set your goals ridiculously high and it's a failure,
you will fail above everyone else's success.
—JAMES CAMERON

•

"Success usually comes to those who are too busy to be looking for it."
—HENRY DAVID THOREAU

•

Entrepreneurs average 3.8 failures before final success. What
sets the successful ones apart is their amazing persistence.
—LISA M. AMOS

If you are not willing to risk the usual, you
will have to settle for the ordinary.
—JIM ROHN

Take up one idea. Make that one idea your life—think of
it, dream of it, live on that idea. Let the brain, muscles,
nerves, every part of your body, be full of that idea, and just
leave every other idea alone. This is the way to success.
—SWAMI VIVEKANANDA

"How far you go in life depends on your being tender with
the young, compassionate with the aged, sympathetic with
the striving, and tolerant of the weak and strong. Because
someday in your life you will have been all of these."
—GEORGE WASHINGTON CARVER

Resentment is one burden that is incompatible with your success.
Always be the first to forgive; and forgive yourself first always.
—DAN ZADRA

Six essential qualities that are the key to success: sincerity,
personal integrity, humility, courtesy, wisdom, charity.
—WILLIAM MENNINGER

The only failure is not to try.
—GEORGE CLOONEY

"If at first you do succeed, try to hide your astonishment."
—ANONYMOUS

Success and rest don't sleep together.
— RUSSIAN PROVERB

"The road to wisdom? Well, it's plain and simple to express:
Err and err and err again, but less and less and less."
— PIET HEIN

Stop chasing the money and start chasing the passion.
— TONY HSIEH

All our dreams can come true if we have the courage to pursue them.
— WALT DISNEY

"He has achieved success who has lived well, laughed often, and loved much; who has enjoyed the trust of pure women, the respect of intelligent men, and the love of little children; who has filled his niche and accomplished his task; who has left the world better than he found it, whether by an improved poppy, a perfect poem, or a rescued soul; who has never lacked appreciation of Earth's beauty or failed to express it; who has always looked for the best in others and given them the best he had; whose life was an inspiration; whose memory a benediction."

—BETTY ANDERSON STANLEY
(often attributed in a somewhat different form to Ralph Waldo Emerson)

Here's what would be pitiful . . .
if your income grew and you didn't.

—JIM ROHN

With money in your pocket, you are wise and you
are handsome and you sing well too.
—YIDDISH PROVERB

Success? I don't know what that word means. I'm happy. But
success, that goes back to what in somebody's eyes success means.
For me, success is inner peace. That's a good day for me.
—DENZEL WASHINGTON

"People who work sitting down get paid more
than people who work standing up."
—OGDEN NASH

Dishonest money dwindles away, but he who
gathers money little by little makes it grow.
—PROVERBS 13:11

Remember that money is of the prolific, generating nature. Money can beget money, and its offspring can beget more, and so on.
—**BENJAMIN FRANKLIN**

The best revenge is massive success.
—**FRANK SINATRA**

I have not failed. I've just found 10,000 ways that won't work.
—**THOMAS EDISON**

A successful man is one who can lay a firm foundation with the bricks others have thrown at him.
—**DAVID BRINKLEY**

Try not to become a man of success, but rather
try to become a man of value.
—ALBERT EINSTEIN

Always bear in mind that your own resolution to success
is more important than any other one thing.
—ABRAHAM LINCOLN

Successful and unsuccessful people do not vary greatly in their
abilities. They vary in their desires to reach their potential.
—JOHN C. MAXWELL

Double your rate of failure. You are thinking of failure as the enemy
of success. But it isn't at all. You can be discouraged by failure or
you can learn from it, so go ahead and make mistakes. Make all
you can. Because remember that's where you will find success.
—THOMAS J. WATSON

Logic will get you from A to B.

Imagination will take you everywhere.

—ALBERT EINSTEIN

"Money often costs too much."

—RALPH WALDO EMERSON

For the love of money is the root of all evil: which while

some coveted after, they have erred from the faith, and

pierced themselves through with many sorrows.

—TIMOTHY 6:10

You cannot motivate the best people with money.

Money is just a way to keep score. The best people

in any field are motivated by passion.

—ERIC S. RAYMOND

If you want to know what a man is really like,

notice how he acts when he loses money.

—SPANISH PROVERB

No one can make you feel inferior without your consent.

—ELEANOR ROOSEVELT

The whole secret of a successful life is to find out

what is one's destiny to do, and then do it.

—HENRY FORD

If you're going through hell, keep going.

—WINSTON CHURCHILL

What seems to us as bitter trials are often blessings in disguise.
—**OSCAR WILDE**

The distance between insanity and genius
is measured only by success.
—**BRUCE FEIRSTEIN**

"Never work just for money or for power.
They won't save your soul or help you sleep at night."
—**MARIAN WRIGHT EDELMAN**

There are no pockets in a shroud.
—**ANONYMOUS**

Beware of little expenses. A small leak will sink a great ship.
— BENJAMIN FRANKLIN

"It's good to have money and the things that money
can buy, but it's good, too, to make sure you haven't
lost the things that money can't buy."
— GEORGE HORACE LORIMER

Annual income twenty pounds,
annual expenditure nineteen six,
result happiness.
Annual income twenty pounds,
annual expenditure twenty pounds ought and six,
result misery.
— MR. MICAWBER, FROM *DAVID COPPERFIELD*,
CHARLES DICKENS

Don't be afraid to give up the good to go for the great.
—JOHN D. ROCKEFELLER

Happiness is a butterfly, which when pursued,
is always beyond your grasp, but which, if you will
sit down quietly, may alight upon you.
—NATHANIEL HAWTHORNE

Resolve not to be poor: whatever you have, spend less.
Poverty is a great enemy to human happiness;
it certainly destroys liberty, and it makes some virtues
impracticable, and others extremely difficult.
—SAMUEL JOHNSON

Buy land. They ain't making any more of the stuff.
—WILL ROGERS

It isn't necessary to be rich and famous to be happy.

It's only necessary to be rich.

—ALAN ALDA

"Being rich is having money; being wealthy is having time."

—STEPHEN SWID

Never spend your money before you have it.

—THOMAS JEFFERSON

I've never been poor, only broke. Being poor is a frame

of mind. Being broke is only a temporary situation.

—MIKE TODD

Motivation is what gets you started. Habit is what keeps you going.

—JIM RYUN

Our greatest fear should not be of failure . . . but of
succeeding at things in life that don't really matter.
—FRANCIS CHAN

Always borrow money from a pessimist.
He doesn't expect to be paid back.
—ANONYMOUS

If you don't design your own life plan, chances are
you'll fall into someone else's plan. And guess what
they have planned for you? Not much.
—JIM ROHN

Nobody ever wrote down a plan to be broke, fat, lazy, or stupid.
Those things are what happen when you don't have a plan.
—LARRY WINGET

Be patient with yourself. Self-growth is tender; it's
holy ground. There's no greater investment.
—STEPHEN R. COVEY

I owe my success to having listened respectfully to the very best
advice, and then going away and doing the exact opposite.
—GILBERT K. CHESTERTON

Be content to act, and leave the talking to others.
—BALTASAR

The greater the artist, the greater the doubt. Perfect confidence
is granted to the less talented as a consolation prize.
—ROBERT HUGHES

What would you attempt to do if you knew you would not fail?

—ROBERT SCHULLER

Remember this saying, "The good paymaster is lord of another man's purse." He that is known to pay punctually and exactly to the time he promises may at any time and on any occasion raise all the money his friends can spare.

—BENJAMIN FRANKLIN

Where large sums of money are concerned, it is advisable to trust nobody.

—AGATHA CHRISTIE

Aim for success, not perfection. Never give up your right to be wrong, because then you will lose the ability to learn new things and move forward with your life. Remember that fear always lurks behind perfectionism.

—DAVID M. BURNS

It is better to fail in originality than to succeed in imitation.

—HERMAN MELVILLE

I cannot give you the formula for success, but I can give you the formula for failure, which is: Try to please everybody.

—HERBERT SWOPE

Screw it, let's just do it.

—RICHARD BRANSON

The ones who are crazy enough to think they can change the world, are the ones that do.

—ANONYMOUS

Success seems to be connected with action. Successful people keep moving. They make mistakes, but they don't quit.

—CONRAD HILTON

The difference between who you are and who
you want to be is what you do.
—UNKNOWN

I failed my way to success.
—THOMAS EDISON

Keep on going, and the chances are that you will stumble on
something, perhaps when you are least expecting it. I never
heard of anyone ever stumbling on something sitting down.
—CHARLES F. KETTERING

Arriving at one goal is the starting point to another.
—JOHN DEWEY

If the highest aim of a captain were to preserve
his ship, he would keep it in port forever.
—THOMAS AQUINAS

Life is like a dogsled team. If you ain't the lead
dog, the scenery never changes.
—LEWIS GRIZZARD

The very essence of leadership is that you have to have vision.
You can't blow an uncertain trumpet.
—THEODORE M. HESBURGH

Always drink upstream from the herd.
—WILL ROGERS

Success in almost any field depends more on energy
and drive than it does on intelligence. This explains
why we have so many stupid leaders.
—SLOAN WILSON

When I finally got a management position, I found
out how hard it is to lead and manage people.
—**GUY KAWASAKI**

The most effective way to do it, is to do it.
—**AMELIA EARHART**

Do not wait until the conditions are perfect to begin.
Beginning makes the conditions perfect.
—**ALAN COHEN**

There is always room at the top.
—**DANIEL WEBSTER**

Chapter Five

■ ■ ■ ■ ■ ■ ■ ■

Bait with Your Heart

{Advice on Friendship, Love,
Marriage, and Other Such Mysteries}

There is love enough in this world for
everybody, if people will just look.
—KURT VONNEGUT

A smart girl leaves before she is left.
—MARILYN MONROE

When you fish for love, bait with your heart, not your brain.
—MARK TWAIN

The best proof of love is trust.
—DR. JOYCE BROTHERS

You'll never forget your first lover, so try to make it someone

you won't regret thinking about for the rest of your life.

—DR. RUTH WESTHEIMER

All you need is love. But a little chocolate now and then doesn't hurt.

—CHARLES SCHULZ

"Never play cards with a man called Doc.

Never eat at a place called Mom's.

Never sleep with a woman whose troubles

are worse than your own."

—NELSON ALGREN

You know it's love when all you want is that person

to be happy, even if you're not part of their happiness.

—JULIA ROBERTS

Do not walk behind me; I may not lead. Do not walk in front of me; I may not follow. Walk beside me, that we may be as one.

—UTE SAYING

For marriage to be a success, every woman and every man should have her and his own bathroom. The end.

—CATHERINE ZETA-JONES

"Keep your eyes wide open before marriage, half shut afterwards."

—BENJAMIN FRANKLIN

Love takes off masks that we fear we cannot live without and know we cannot live within.

—JAMES BALDWIN

As long as you know that most men

are like children, you know everything.

—COCO CHANEL

The quickest way to know a woman is to go shopping with her.

—MARCELENE COX

By all means, marry. If you get a good wife,

you'll become happy; if you get a bad one,

you'll become a philosopher.

—SOCRATES

Love yourself first and everything else falls into line. You really

have to love yourself to get anything done in this world.

—LUCILLE BALL

The most important thing in life is to learn how
to give out love, and to let it come in.
—MORRIE SCHWARTZ

Never advise anyone to go to war or to marry.
—SPANISH PROVERB

In buying a horse and taking a wife, shut your
eyes and commend yourself to God.
—ITALIAN PROVERB

"Never close your lips to those whom you have opened your heart."
—CHARLES DICKENS

The quality of a relationship is a function of the extent
to which it is built on a solid underlying friendship and
meets the needs of the two people involved.

—DR. PHIL MCGRAW

If I know what love is, it is because of you.

—HERMAN HESSE

I love you not because of who you are, but because
of who I am when I am with you.

—ROY CROFT

Love is a friendship set to music.

—JOSEPH CAMPBELL

"It doesn't matter if the guy is perfect or the girl is perfect, as long as they are perfect for each other."

—FROM THE FILM *GOOD WILL HUNTING*
(Matt Damon and Ben Affleck, screenwriters)

'Tis better to have loved and lost
Than never to have loved at all.

—ALFRED, LORD TENNYSON

A successful marriage is an edifice that must be rebuilt every day.

—ANDRÉ MAUROIS

We are shaped and fashioned by what we love.

—JOHANN WOLFGANG VON GOETHE

The way to love anything is to realize that it may be lost.

—GILBERT K. CHESTERTON

•

It takes courage to love, but pain through love is the purifying fire which those who love generously know. We all know people who are so much afraid of pain that they shut themselves up like clams in a shell and, giving out nothing, receive nothing and therefore shrink until life is a mere living death.

—ELEANOR ROOSEVELT

•

Love sought is good, but given unsought, is better.

**—OLIVIA, FROM *TWELFTH NIGHT*,
WILLIAM SHAKESPEARE**

He was my North, my South, my East and West,

My working week and my Sunday rest,

My noon, my midnight, my talk, my song;

I thought that love would last forever: I was wrong.

—W. H. AUDEN

We cannot really love anybody with whom we never laugh.

—AGNES REPPLIER

"Love is like a flower: Once you pick it, it slowly dies."

—ANONYMOUS

"If you want to sacrifice the admiration of many men

for the criticism of one, go ahead, get married."

—KATHARINE HEPBURN

You can rehearse a wedding but not a marriage.
—AL BATT

Don't brood. Get on with living and loving. You don't have forever.
—LEO BUSCAGLIA

Your task is not to seek for love, but merely to seek and find all
the barriers within yourself that you have built against it.
—RUMI

Love is of all passions the strongest, for it attacks
simultaneously the head, the heart and the senses.
—LAO-TZU

Never pretend to a love which you do not actually
feel, for love is not ours to command.
—**ALAN WATTS**

"Once the realization is accepted that even between the closest human
beings infinite distances continue, a wonderful living side by side
can grow, if they succeed in loving the distance between them which
makes it possible for each to see the other whole against the sky."
—**RAINER MARIA RILKE**

I'm old-fashioned and a square. I believe people should not engage
in sex too early. They will never forget that first sexual experience,
and it would be a pity to just throw it away. So what's the rush? Hug
and kiss and neck and pet, and don't rush into a sexual encounter.
—**DR. RUTH WESTHEIMER**

It is better to be looked over than overlooked.

—MAE WEST

•

"Do not let too strong a light come into your bedroom.
There are in a beauty a great many things which are
enhanced by being seen only in a half-light."

—OVID

•

At the touch of love everyone becomes a poet.

—PLATO

•

If I had a flower for every time I thought of you . . .
I could walk through my garden forever.

—ALFRED, LORD TENNYSON

It doesn't make any difference what you do in the bedroom as long as you don't do it in the street and frighten the horses.
—MRS. PATRICK CAMPBELL

The best and most beautiful things in this world cannot be seen or even heard, but must be felt with the heart.
—HELEN KELLER

Keep love in your heart. A life without it is like a sunless garden when the flowers are dead.
—OSCAR WILDE

I believe that love cannot be bought except with love.
—JOHN STEINBECK

Marriage has no guarantees. If that's what you're
looking for, go live with a car battery.

—ERMA BOMBECK

Immature love says: "I love you because I need you."
Mature love says: "I need you because I love you."

—ERICH FROMM

You know you're in love when you don't want to fall asleep
because reality is finally better than your dreams.

—DR. SEUSS (THEODOR GEISEL)

Life without love is like a tree without blossoms or fruit.

—KHALIL GIBRAN

"Love is everything it's cracked up to be . . .
It really is worth fighting for, being brave for,
risking everything for."
—ERICA JONG

For women the best aphrodisiacs are words. The G-spot is in
the ears. He who looks for it below there is wasting his time.
—ISABEL ALLENDE

I have decided to stick with love. Hate is too great a burden to bear.
—MARTIN LUTHER KING JR.

We are most alive when we're in love.
—JOHN UPDIKE

A kiss is a lovely trick designed by nature to stop
speech when words become superfluous.
—INGRID BERGMAN

All married couples should learn the art of battle as they should
learn the art of making love. Good battle is objective and honest,
never vicious or cruel. Good battle is healthy and constructive,
and brings to a marriage the principle of equal partnership.
—ANN LANDERS

When angry, count ten before you speak; if very angry, a hundred.
—THOMAS JEFFERSON

Love is a better teacher than duty.
—ALBERT EINSTEIN

True love comes quietly, without banners or flashing lights. If you hear bells, get your ears checked.
—ERICH SEGAL

Every person has to love at least one bad partner in their lives to be truly thankful for the right one.
—UNKNOWN

"When angry, count to four; when very angry, swear."
—MARK TWAIN

While forbidden fruit is said to taste sweeter, it usually spoils faster.
—ABIGAIL VAN BUREN ("DEAR ABBY")

Don't criticize in the sack. Discuss constructively later.
— **DR. RUTH WESTHEIMER**

If you think marriage is going to be perfect,

you're probably still at your reception.
— **MARTHA BOLTON**

"Remember, we all stumble, every one of us.

That's why it's a comfort to go hand in hand."
— **EMILY KIMBROUGH**

Friendship . . . is not something you learn in school.

But if you haven't learned the meaning of friendship,

you really haven't learned anything.
— **MUHAMMAD ALI**

Fortune and love favor the brave.

—OVID

•

Love never dies a natural death. It dies because
we don't know how to replenish its source.
It dies of blindness and errors and betrayals.
It dies of illness and wounds; it dies of weariness,
of witherings, of tarnishings.

—ANAÏS NIN

•

If you live to be a hundred, I want to live to be a hundred
minus one day so I never have to live without you.

—A. A. MILNE

A true apology is more than just acknowledgment of a mistake. It is recognition that something you have said or done has damaged a relationship and that you care enough about the relationship to want it repaired and restored.
—NORMAN VINCENT PEALE

Grief can take care of itself, but to get the full value of a joy you must have somebody to divide it with.
—MARK TWAIN

If you can, help others; if you cannot do that, at least do not harm them.
—TENZIN GYATSO, 14TH DALAI LAMA

"Friendship is the only cement that will ever hold the world together."
—WOODROW WILSON

The most important thing in life is giving back.
—MICHAEL R. BLOOMBERG

I'll tell you the same thing my mother used to tell me:
"The most important thing in life is to try to do the very
best for your neighbors. Respect other people."
—HANK AARON

Be respectful to others as you grow . . . If we lack respect for one
group, then there is a tendency for that attitude to spread. It becomes
infectious and no one becomes safe from the ravages of prejudice.
—WALTER ANNENBERG

Distrust all those who love you extremely upon a very
slight acquaintance and without any visible reason.
—LORD CHESTERFIELD

"Thy friend has a friend,
and thy friend's friend has
a friend; be discreet."
—THE TALMUD

Every human being has value. This is the basis of all healthy
relationships. Through living each day as it is given to me,
I've learned that. It cannot be "taught," but it can be "caught"
from those who live their lives right along with us.
—FRED ROGERS ("MR. ROGERS")

The real test of friendship is:

can you literally do nothing with the other person?

Can you enjoy those moments of life that are utterly simple?

—EUGENE KENNEDY

Santa Claus has the right idea. Visit people only once a year.

—VICTOR BORGE

"Laughter is not at all a bad beginning for a friendship,

and it is far the best ending for one."

—OSCAR WILDE

Do not keep on with a mockery of friendship after the

substance is gone—but part, while you can part friends. Bury

the carcass of friendship: it is not worth embalming.

—WILLIAM HAZLITT

Some people think only intellect counts: knowing how to solve problems, knowing how to get by, knowing how to identify an advantage and seize it. But the functions of intellect are insufficient without courage, love, friendship, compassion, and empathy.

—DEAN KOONTZ

"All love that has not friendship for its base,
is like a mansion built upon the sand."

—ELLA WHEELER WILCOX

You shall judge a man by his foes as well as by his friends.

—JOSEPH CONRAD

"It takes a long time to grow an old friend."

—JOHN LEONARD

It's the little things that matter, that add up in the end,
with the priceless thrilling magic found only in a friend.
—ELIZABETH DUNPHY

The first duty of love is to listen.
—PAUL TILLICH

"Never assume, for it makes an ASS out of U and ME."
—ANONYMOUS

Fish and visitors stink after three days.
—BENJAMIN FRANKLIN

I tell you, the more I think, the more I feel that there is
nothing more truly artistic than to love people.
—VINCENT VAN GOGH

Hatred paralyzes life; love releases it.
Hatred confuses life; love harmonizes it.
Hatred darkens life; love illuminates it.
—MARTIN LUTHER KING JR.

Love doesn't just sit there, like a stone;
it has to be made, like bread,
remade all the time, made new.
—URSULA K. LE GUIN

Love is not enough. It must be the foundation, the cornerstone—but
not the complete structure. It is much too pliable, too yielding.
—BETTE DAVIS

•

Spread love everywhere you go. Let no one ever
come to you without leaving happier.
—MOTHER TERESA

•

Never miss an opportunity to make others happy,
even if you have to leave them alone in order to do it.
—ANONYMOUS

•

"Always be nice to your children, because they are
the ones who will choose your rest home."
—PHYLLIS DILLER

Never raise your hand to your kids.

It leaves your groin unprotected.

—RED BUTTONS

Always serve too much hot fudge sauce on hot fudge sundaes.

It makes people overjoyed, and puts them in your debt.

—JUDITH OLNEY

"There is no remedy for love but to love more."

—HENRY DAVID THOREAU

It is not self-sacrifice to die protecting that which you value:

If the value is great enough, you do not care to exist without

it. This applies to any alleged sacrifice for those one loves.

—AYN RAND

Love one another and you will be happy.
It's as simple and as difficult as that.
— MICHAEL LEUNIG

The truth is that there is only one terminal dignity—
love. And the story of a love is not important—what
is important is that one is capable of love. It is perhaps
the only glimpse we are permitted of eternity.
— HELEN HAYES

"You have to love your children unselfishly.
That's hard. But it's the only way."
— BARBARA BUSH

If someone is too tired to give you a smile, leave one of your own,
because no one needs a smile as much as those who have none to give.
—**RABBI SAMSON HIRSCH**

Love yourself first and everything else falls into line. You really
have to love yourself to get anything done in this world.
—**LUCILLE BALL**

The most important thing a father can do for
his children is to love their mother.
—**THEODORE M. HESBURGH**

"The most important things to do in the world are to get something
to eat, something to drink, and somebody to love you."
—**BRENDAN BEHAN**

A total immersion in life offers the best classroom for learning to love.
—LEO BUSCAGLIA

If you wish to be loved, show more of your faults than your virtues.
—EDWARD BULWER-LYTTON

Until one has loved an animal, a part of
one's soul remains unawakened.
—ANATOLE FRANCE

"There is only misfortune in not being loved;
there is misery in not loving."
—ALBERT CAMUS

If you cannot work with love but only with distaste,

it is better that you should leave your work.

—KAHLIL GIBRAN

•

"Assist the reduced fellow man, either by a considerable gift or a sum of money or by teaching him a trade or by putting him in the way of business so that he may earn an honest livelihood and not be forced to the dreadful alternative of holding out his hand for charity. This is the highest step and summit of charity's golden ladder."

—MOSES MAIMONIDES

•

"If you have only one smile in you, give it to the people you love. Don't be surly at home, then go out in the street and start grinning 'Good morning' at total strangers."

—MAYA ANGELOU

We love the things we love for what they are.

—ROBERT FROST

Only time can heal your broken heart, just as only

time can heal his broken arms and legs.

—MISS PIGGY

It's better to be unhappy alone than unhappy with someone.

—MARILYN MONROE

The greater your capacity to love, the greater

your capacity to feel the pain.

—JENNIFER ANISTON

Hearts will never be practical until they are made unbreakable.

—WIZARD OF OZ

To be brave is to love unconditionally without
expecting anything in return.

—MADONNA

You don't marry someone you can live with—
you marry the person who you cannot live without.

—UNKNOWN

Love is just a word, but you bring it definition.

—EMINEM

When you break up, your whole identity is shattered. It's like death.

—DENNIS QUAID

And in the end, the love you take is equal to the love you make.

—PAUL MCCARTNEY

Love is composed of a single soul inhabiting two bodies.

—ARISTOTLE

•

People are often unreasonable, illogical, and self-centered; Forgive them anyway. If you are kind, people may accuse you of selfish, ulterior motives; Be kind anyway. If you are successful, you will win some false friends and some true enemies; Succeed anyway. If you are honest and frank, people may cheat you; Be honest and frank anyway. What you spend years building, someone could destroy overnight; Build anyway. If you find serenity and happiness, they may be jealous; Be happy anyway. The good you do today, people will often forget tomorrow; Do good anyway. Give the world the best you have, and it may never be enough; Give the world the best you have got anyway. You see, in the final analysis, it is between you and God; It was never between you and them anyway.

—MOTHER TERESA

Chapter Six

■ ■ ■ ■ ■ ■ ■ ■ ■

Throw Your Dreams

{Advice to Inspire and Encourage}

Your greatest fears are created by your
imagination. Don't give in to them.
—WINSTON CHURCHILL

Get a cocktail shaker.
—JOSÉ ANDRÉS

Ban self-doubt.
—JENNIFER LEE

You can't connect the dots looking forward.
—STEVE JOBS

The world is more malleable than you think.

—BONO

Throw your dreams into space like a kite,

and you do not know what it will bring back;

a new life, a new friend, a new love, a new country.

—ANAÏS NIN

If you can dream it, you can do it.

—WALT DISNEY

We must accept finite disappointment, but

we must never lose infinite hope.

—MARTIN LUTHER KING JR.

We must embrace pain and burn it as fuel for our journey.
—KENJI MIYAZAWA

One of the things I learned the hard way was that it doesn't
pay to get discouraged. Keeping busy and making optimism
a way of life can restore your faith in yourself.
—LUCILLE BALL

Be yourself. The world worships the original.
—INGRID BERGMAN

Be careful what you set your heart upon—for it will surely be yours.
—JAMES BALDWIN

What counts can't always be counted; what
can be counted doesn't always count.
—**ALBERT EINSTEIN**

The secret of life is in opening up your heart.
—**CHITA RIVERA**

Sometimes our light goes out, but is blown again into instant
flame by an encounter with another human being.
—**ALBERT SCHWEITZER**

You can learn new things at any time in your life if you're
willing to be a beginner. If you actually learn to like
being a beginner, the whole world opens up to you.
—**BARBARA SHER**

"Don't be a blueprint.

Be an original."

—ROY ACUFF

•

Most of the important things in the world have been
accomplished by people who have kept on trying
when there seemed to be no hope at all.

—DALE CARNEGIE

•

I slept and dreamt that life was joy. I awoke and saw that
life was service. I acted and behold, service was joy.

—RABINDRANATH TAGORE

We should always pray for help, but we should always
listen for inspiration and impression to proceed in ways
different from those we may have thought of.
— JOHN H. GROBERG

A problem is a chance for you to do your best.
— DUKE ELLINGTON

When everything seems to be going against you, remember
that the airplane takes off against the wind, not with it.
— HENRY FORD

Indulge your imagination in every possible flight.
— JANE AUSTEN

Only those who will risk going too far can

possibly find out how far one can go.

—T. S. ELIOT

Life is good only when it is magical and musical, a perfect
timing and consent, and when we do not anatomise it. You
must treat the days respectfully . . . You must hear the bird's
song without attempting to render it into nouns and verbs.

—RALPH WALDO EMERSON

"A ship in port is safe, but that's not what ships are built for."

—GRACE HOPPER

Disappointment should be cremated, not embalmed.

—HENRY S. HASKINS

When one door closes, another opens; but we often
look so long and so regretfully upon the closed door that
we do not see the one which has opened for us.
—**HELEN KELLER**

Obstacles don't have to stop you. If you run into a
wall, don't turn around and give up. Figure out how
to climb it, go through it, or work around it.
—**MICHAEL JORDAN**

Problems are not stop signs, they are guidelines.
—**ROBERT SCHULLER**

"A man, as a general rule, owes very little to what he is born with—a man is what he makes of himself."
—ALEXANDER GRAHAM BELL

Shoot for the moon. Even if you miss, you'll land among the stars.
—LES BROWN

Our greatest glory is not in never failing, but in rising up every time we fail.
—RALPH WALDO EMERSON

Those who contemplate the beauty of the earth find reserves of strength that will endure as long as life lasts.
—RACHEL CARSON

Hope is important because it can make the present
moment less difficult to bear. If we believe that tomorrow
will be better, we can bear a hardship today.
—THICH NHAT HANH

•

The difference between stumbling blocks and
stepping stones is how you use them.
—UNKNOWN

•

"The most worthwhile thing is to try to put
happiness into the lives of others."
—SIR ROBERT BADEN-POWELL

"Each time a man stands up for an ideal, or acts to improve the lot of others, or strikes out against injustice, he sends forth a tiny ripple of hope, and crossing each other from a million different centers of energy and daring, those ripples build a current that can sweep down the mightiest walls of oppression and resistance."

—ROBERT F. KENNEDY

Resolve to be thyself: and know, that he who finds himself, loses his misery.

—MATTHEW ARNOLD

Always remember that the future comes one day at a time.

—DEAN ACHESON

For the past thirty-three years, I have looked in the mirror
every morning and asked myself, "If today were the last day
of my life, would I want to do what I am about to do today?"
And whenever the answer has been "No" for too many
days in a row, I know I need to change something.

—STEVE JOBS

Quit now, you'll never make it. If you disregard
this advice, you'll be halfway there.

—DAVID ZUCKER

"There are only two lasting legacies we can hope to give
our children. One of these is roots; the other, wings."

—HODDING CARTER

We make a living by what we get,

but we make a life by what we give.

—WINSTON CHURCHILL

Next to trying and winning, the best thing is trying and failing.

—L. M. MONTGOMERY

The only true gift is a portion of yourself.

—RALPH WALDO EMERSON

"Waste no more time arguing what a good man should be. Be one."

—MARCUS AURELIUS

Do something for somebody every day for which you do not get paid.

—**ALBERT SCHWEITZER**

Only a life lived in the service of others is worth living.

—**ALBERT EINSTEIN**

"Remember always that you have not only the right to be
an individual, you have an obligation to be one. You cannot
make any useful contribution in life unless you do this."

—**ELEANOR ROOSEVELT**

Just as despair can come to one only from other human beings,
hope, too, can be given to one only by other human beings.

—**ELIE WEISEL**

The greatest glory in living lies not in never
failing, but in rising every time we fail.
—NELSON MANDELA

In times of great stress or adversity, it's always best to keep busy,
to plow your anger and your energy into something positive.
—LEE IACOCCA

Thank God—every morning when you get up—that you have
something to do which must be done, whether you like it or
not. Being forced to work, and forced to do your best, will breed
in you a hundred virtues which the idle will never know.
—CHARLES KINGSLEY

Be yourself.

Who else is better qualified?

—FRANK J. GIBLIN II

Life consists not in holding good cards

but in playing those you hold well.

—JOSH BILLINGS

It is only in our darkest hours that we may discover

the true strength of the brilliant light within ourselves

that can never, ever, be dimmed.

—DOE ZANTAMATA

If it's not exactly like you thought it would be, you think it's

a failure. What about the spectrum of colors in between.

—SARA EVANS

Use what you've been through as fuel, believe
in yourself and be unstoppable!
—YVONNE PIERRE

Don't be afraid your life will end;
be afraid that it will never begin.
—GRACE HANSEN

Begin doing what you want to do now. We are not living
in eternity. We have only this moment, sparkling like a
star in our hand—and melting like a snowflake.
—SIR FRANCIS BACON

The best remedy for those who are afraid, lonely, or
unhappy is to go outside, somewhere where they can be
quiet, alone with the heavens, nature and God.
—ANNE FRANK

Tranquility is like quicksilver. The harder you
grab for it, the less likely you will grasp it.
— BERN WILLIAMS

"Three grand essentials to happiness in this life are something
to do, something to love, and something to hope for."
— JOSEPH ADDISON

To give pleasure to a single heart by a single kind act is
better than a thousand headbowings in prayer.
— SAADI

There are three ingredients to the good life:
learning, earning, and yearning.
— CHRISTOPHER MORLEY

It is difficult to steer a parked car, so get moving.
—**HENRIETTA MEARS**

●

Labor to keep alive in your breast that little
spark of celestial fire called conscience.
—**GEORGE WASHINGTON**

●

There is a way to look at the past. Don't hide from
it. It will not catch you if you don't repeat it.
—**PEARL BAILEY**

●

"You must learn day by day, year by year, to broaden your
horizon. The more things you love, the more you are interested
in, the more you enjoy, the more you are indignant about,
the more you have left when anything happens."
—**ETHEL BARRYMORE**

Better keep yourself clean and bright; you are the
window through which you must see the world.
— GEORGE BERNARD SHAW

•

Seize the moment. Remember all those women on
the *Titanic* who waved off the dessert cart.
— ERMA BOMBECK

•

To help yourself, help others. Whatever good you do travels
a circle and returns to you many times over—but remember,
life isn't about what you get, it's about what you become.
— DENNIS GASKILL

•

"Look up and not down. Look forward and not back.
Look out and not in, and lend a hand."
— EDWARD EVERETT HALE

It is folly for a man to pray to the gods for that which
he has the power to obtain by himself.
—EPICURUS

Dwell not on the past. Use it to illustrate a point, then leave it
behind. Nothing really matters except what you do now in this
instant of time. From this moment onwards you can be an entirely
different person, filled with love and understanding, ready with an
outstretched hand, uplifted and positive in every thought and deed.
—EILEEN CADDY

Your children need your presence more than your presents.
—JESSE JACKSON

You must be the change you wish to see in the world.
—**MOHANDAS GANDHI**

•

Do, or do not. There is no "try."
—**YODA,** *THE EMPIRE STRIKES BACK*
(screenplay by Leigh Brackett and Lawrence Kasdan)

•

Everybody can be great . . . because anybody can serve. You don't have to have a college degree to serve. You don't have to make your subject and verb agree to serve. . . . You only need a heart full of grace. A soul generated by love.
—**MARTIN LUTHER KING JR.**

"Whenever you feel the need or wish to cheer yourself, think about all of the good qualities of those around you—the energy of one, for instance, the modesty of another, the generosity of a third, and some other gift of a fourth. For nothing is ever so cheering as the images of the qualities shining through in the character of those who live with us. . . . Have these images then ever before your eyes."
—MARCUS AURELIUS

Treat a man as if he were what he ought to be and you help him become what he is capable of being.
—JOHANN VON GOETHE

Don't compromise yourself.
You're all you've got.
—JANIS JOPLIN

Carry out a random act of kindness,

with no expectation of reward, safe in the knowledge

that one day someone might do the same for you.

—PRINCESS DIANA

Do not look where you fell, but where you slipped.

—ANONYMOUS

"God, grant me the serenity

to accept the things I cannot change;

courage to change the things I can;

and wisdom to know the difference."

—DR. REINHOLD NIEBUHR

(THE SERENITY PRAYER)

If your daily life seems poor, do not blame it; blame yourself, tell yourself that you are not poet enough to call forth its riches.
—**RAINER MARIA RILKE**

Share and save the world.
—**MAITREYA**

"Act the way you'd like to be and soon you'll be the way you act."
—**GEORGE W. CRANE**

I learned there are troubles of more than one kind. Some come from ahead, others come from behind. But I've bought a big bat. I'm all ready, you see. Now my troubles are going to have trouble with me.

—DR. SEUSS (THEODOR GEISEL)

In three words I can sum up everything I've learned about life. It goes on.

—ROBERT FROST

If you want a quality, act as if you already had it.

—WILLIAM JAMES

Jack Kennedy always said to me, "Hedy, get involved.

That's the secret of life. Try everything.

Join everything. Meet everybody."

—HEDY LAMARR

If you really want something in this life, you have to work for it.

Now, quiet, they're about to announce the lottery numbers!

—HOMER SIMPSON, *THE SIMPSONS*,

MATT GROENING

Believe that life is worth living and your belief will help create the fact.

—WILLIAM JAMES

Have great hopes and dare to go all out for them.
Have great dreams and dare to live them. Have
tremendous expectations and believe in them.
—NORMAN VINCENT PEALE

Things turn out the best for the people who make
the best of the way things turn out.
—JOHN WOODEN

If you pray for a Cadillac and God sends a jackass, ride it.
—ANONYMOUS

Know yourself. Don't accept your dog's admiration as
conclusive evidence that you are wonderful.
—ANN LANDERS

The best way to get rid of the pain is to feel the pain. And
when you feel the pain and go beyond it, you'll see there's
a very intense love that is wanting to awaken itself.
—DEEPAK CHOPRA

Man is fond of counting his troubles but he does not count
his joys. If he counted them up, as he ought to, he would
see that every lot has enough happiness provided for it.
—FYODOR DOSTOEVSKY

Be who you are and say what you feel, because those who
mind don't matter, and those who matter don't mind.
—DR. SEUSS (THEODOR GEISEL)

Don't wait for the last judgment—it takes place every day.
—ALBERT CAMUS

Remember your humanity, and forget the rest.
—BERTRAND RUSSELL

When things are bad, we take comfort in the thought that they could always get worse. And when they are, we find hope in the thought that things are so bad they have to get better.
—MALCOLM FORBES

He knows not his own strength who hath not met adversity.
—WILLIAM SAMUEL JOHNSON

Look at a day when you are supremely satisfied at the end.
It's not a day when you lounge around doing nothing; it's
when you've had everything to do, and you've done it.
—**LORD ACTON**

"Finish each day and be done with it. You have done what you could;
some blunders and absurdities have crept in; forget them as soon
as you can. Tomorrow is a new day; you shall begin it serenely and
with too high a spirit to be encumbered with your old nonsense."
—**RALPH WALDO EMERSON**

You can't wait for inspiration. You have to go after it with a club.
—**JACK LONDON**

Life is like photography. You need the negatives to develop.

—UNKNOWN

Life isn't about finding yourself. Life is about creating yourself.

—GEORGE BERNARD SHAW

Never be bullied into silence. Never allow yourself to be made a victim. Accept no one's definition of your life; define yourself.

—HARVEY FIERSTEIN

The price of anything is the amount of life you exchange for it.
—HENRY DAVID THOREAU

Twenty years from now you will be more disappointed
by the things that you didn't do than by the ones you
did do. So throw off the bowlines. Catch the trade
winds in your sails. Explore. Dream. Discover.
—MARK TWAIN

Don't judge each day by the harvest you
reap but by the seeds you plant.
—ROBERT LOUIS STEVENSON

Chapter Seven

Hit the Right Keys

{Advice on Creativity and the Arts}

The arts are not a way to make a living. They are a very human way of making life more bearable. Practicing an art, no matter how well or badly, is a way to make your soul grow, for heaven's sake.

—KURT VONNEGUT

•

There's nothing remarkable about it. All one has to do is hit the right keys at the right time and the instrument plays itself.

—JOHANN SEBASTIAN BACH

•

"When in doubt, make a fool of yourself. There is a microscopically thin line between being brilliantly creative and acting like the most gigantic idiot on earth. So what the hell, leap!"

—CYNTHIA HEIMEL

Creativity is allowing yourself to make mistakes.

Art is knowing which ones to keep.

—SCOTT ADAMS

Curiosity is the key to creativity.

—AKIO MORITA

If you want to work on your art, work on your life.

—ANTON CHEKHOV

Find a need and fill it.

—RUTH STAFFORD PEALE

A long walk and grooming with a well-mannered dog is a Zen experience that leaves you refreshed and in a creative frame of mind.

—DEAN KOONTZ

You can't depend on your eyes when your imagination is out of focus.

—MARK TWAIN

Marry an English major and get a good editor.

—STEPHEN AMBROSE

"Iron rusts from disuse, stagnant water loses its purity, and in cold weather becomes frozen; even so does inaction sap the vigors of the mind."

—LEONARDO DA VINCI

When a thing has been said, and said well,

have no scruple. Take it and copy it.

—ANATOLE FRANCE

A man's style in any art should be like his dress—

it should attract as little attention as possible.

—SAMUEL BUTLER

Employ in everything a certain casualness which conceals

art and creates the impression that what is done and said is

accomplished without effort and without its being thought about.

It is from this, in my opinion, that grace largely derives.

—BALDASSARE CASTIGLIONE

Do not follow where the path may lead. Go instead
where there is no path and leave a trail.
—MURIEL STRODE

•

"Anyone can make the simple complicated—
creativity is making the complicated simple."
—CHARLES MINGUS

•

Never judge a work of art by its defects.
—WASHINGTON ALLSTON

•

Never pay attention to what critics say. Remember, a
statue has never been set up in honor of a critic.
—JEAN SIBELIUS

"Don't be an art critic, but paint; there lies salvation."
—PAUL CEZANNE

Art is the only thing you cannot punch a button for.
You must do it the old-fashioned way. Stay up and really
burn the midnight oil. There are no compromises.
—LEONTYNE PRICE

"To be truly creative, you have to work beyond what you know.
Pushing the envelope is what being an artist is all about."
—JOHN FERRIE

Take the best that exists and make it better. If it doesn't exist, create it.
—SIR HENRY ROYCE

"Sometimes you've got to let everything go—purge yourself. If you are unhappy with anything . . . whatever is bringing you down, get rid of it. Because you'll find that when you're free, your true creativity, your true self comes out."
—TINA TURNER

Technique alone is never enough. You have to have passion. Technique alone is just an embroidered pot holder.
—RAYMOND CHANDLER

Use what talents you possess: the woods would be very silent
if no birds sang there except those that sang best.
—HENRY VAN DYKE

You should not give anybody the power to decide
what is right and wrong in your creativity.
—ANAÏS NIN

Creativity comes from trust. Trust your instincts.
And never hope more than you work.
—RITA MAE BROWN

Think left and think right and think low and think high.

Oh, the thinks you can think up if only you try!

—DR. SEUSS (THEODOR GEISEL)

"Turn loose and have fun. Give the audience a show."

—ROY ACUFF

Whatever you do, kid, serve it with a little dressing.

—GEORGE M. COHAN (TO SPENCER TRACY)

I believe entertainment can aspire to be art, and can become art, but if you set out to make art you're an idiot.

—STEVE MARTIN

Show business is really 90 percent luck and 10 percent
being able to handle it when it gets offered to you.
—TOMMY STEELE

If you've got talent, stick with it . . .
because talent wins out, without a doubt.
—BOBBY SHERMAN

Actors should be overheard, not listened to, and the
audience is 50 percent of the performance.
—SHIRLEY BOOTH

"'Get out of show business.' It's the best advice I ever
got, because I'm so stubborn that if someone would tell
me that, I would stay in it to the bitter end."
—**WALTER MATTHAU**

"Here's my advice to you young comedians—
live to be old comedians.
I don't see how you can go wrong with that."
—**GEORGE BURNS**

If you haven't struck oil in the first three minutes—stop boring.
—**GEORGE JESSEL**

Chapter Eight

Imitate a Champion

{Advice on Sports and Competition}

Baseball is the only field of endeavor where a man can succeed

three times out of ten and be considered a good performer.

—**TED WILLIAMS**

•

One man practicing sportsmanship is far better than 50 preaching it.

—**KNUTE ROCKNE**

•

The best and fastest way to learn a sport is

to watch and imitate a champion.

—**JEAN-CLAUDE KILLY**

•

Push yourself again and again. Don't give an

inch until the final buzzer sounds.

—**LARRY BIRD**

Nobody in the game of football should be called a genius.

A genius is somebody like Norman Einstein.

— JOE THEISMANN

The first thing is to love your sport. Never do it to

please someone else. It has to be yours.

— PEGGY FLEMING

The race is not always to the swift,

nor the battle to the strong,

but that's the way to bet.

— DAMON RUNYON

Never give up! Failure and rejection are

only the first step to succeeding.

— JIM VALVANO

Age is no barrier. It's a limitation you put on your mind.
—JACKIE JOYNER-KERSEE

"Ask not what your teammates can do for you.
Ask what you can do for your teammates."
—EARVIN "MAGIC" JOHNSON

Warriors take chances. Like everyone else, they fear
failing, but they refuse to let fear control them.
—SAMURAI PROVERB

The greatest efforts in sports come when
the mind is as still as a glass lake.
—W. TIMOTHY GALLWEY

"Luck is the residue of design."
—BRANCH RICKEY

It's not whether you get knocked down; it's whether you get up.
—VINCE LOMBARDI

What you lack in talent can be made up with desire,

hustle, and giving 110 percent all the time.
—DON ZIMMER

Loosen your girdle and let 'er fly!
—BABE DIDRIKSON ZAHARIAS

The highest compliment that you can pay me is to say
that I work hard every day, that I never dog it.
—WAYNE GRETZKY

Gold medals aren't really made of gold. They're made of
sweat, determination, and a hard-to-find alloy called guts.
—DAN GABLE

"Be bold. If you're going to make an error, make a doozy, and don't be afraid to hit the ball."

—BILLIE JEAN KING

It ain't over 'til it's over.

—YOGI BERRA

The only way to prove that you're a good sport is to lose.

—ERNIE BANKS

An acre of performance is worth

a whole world of promise.

—RED AUERBACH

There may be people that have more talent than you, but

there's no excuse for anyone to work harder than you do.

—DEREK JETER

Football is like life—it requires perseverance, self-denial, hard

work, sacrifice, dedication, and respect for authority.

—VINCE LOMBARDI

Competitive sports are played mainly on a five-and-a-half-inch court—the space between your ears.

—BOBBY JONES

"And listen—you've got to kid him. Get his goat. Call him 'hot shot,' 'big britches,' 'smarty pants,' or even 'Toots,' until he gets so nervous he doesn't know which goal is which."

—A COACH'S ADVICE TO A ROOKIE FOOTBALL PLAYER, AS QUOTED IN A 1937 WISCONSIN NEWSPAPER

Show me a guy who's afraid to look bad, and I'll show you a guy you can beat every time.

—LOU BROCK

An athlete cannot run with money in his pockets. He must
run with hope in his heart and dreams in his head.

—EMIL ZATOPEK

Somewhere behind the athlete you've become and the hours of
practice and the coaches who have pushed you is a little girl who
fell in love with the game and never looked back . . . play for her.

—MIA HAMM

When you're riding, only the race in which
you're riding is important.

—BILL SHOEMAKER

Talent wins games, but teamwork and intelligence
win championships.
—**MICHAEL JORDAN**

The way a team plays as a whole determines its success. You may
have the greatest bunch of individual stars in the world, but if
they don't play together, the club won't be worth a dime.
—**BABE RUTH**

A champion is someone who gets up when he can't.
—**JACK DEMPSEY**

Make the hard ones look easy and the easy ones look hard.
—WALTER HAGEN

When you've got something to prove,
there's nothing greater than a challenge.
—TERRY BRADSHAW

"Concentration is the ability to think about absolutely
nothing when it is absolutely necessary."
—RAY KNIGHT

You were born to be a player. You were meant
to be here. This moment is yours.
—HERB BROOKS

The road to Easy Street goes through the sewer.
— **JOHN MADDEN**

How you respond to the challenge in the second half will determine what you become after the game, whether you are a winner or a loser.
— **LOU HOLTZ**

One hundred percent of shots not taken don't go in.
— **WAYNE GRETZKY**

I've always made a total effort, even when the odds seemed entirely against me. I never quit trying; I never felt that I didn't have a chance to win.
— **ARNOLD PALMER**

"My motto was always to keep swinging. Whether I was
in a slump or feeling badly or having trouble off the
field, the only thing to do was keep swinging."
—HANK AARON

You are never really playing an opponent.
You are playing yourself, your own highest standards,
and when you reach your limits, that is real joy.
—ARTHUR ASHE

The more difficult the victory, the greater the happiness in winning.
—PELE

"Being number two sucks."
—ANDRE AGASSI

You can learn a line from a win and a book from a defeat.
—PAUL BROWN

Defeat is worse than death because you have to live with defeat.
—ANONYMOUS

You can't win unless you learn how to lose.
—KAREEM ABDUL-JABBAR

You gotta be careful with your body. Your body is like a bar
of soap. The more you use it, the more it wears down.
—RICHIE ALLEN

•

One man can be a crucial ingredient on a team,
but one man cannot make a team.
—KAREEM ABDUL-JABBAR

•

You've got to take the initiative and play your game.
In a decisive set, confidence is the difference.
—CHRIS EVERT

•

When you win, say nothing, when you lose, say less.
—PAUL BROWN

The mind is the limit. As long as the mind can
envision the fact that you can do something, you can
do it, as long as you really believe 100 percent.
—**ARNOLD SCHWARZENEGGER**

It's not the size of the dog in the fight,
but the size of the fight in the dog.
—**ARCHIE GRIFFIN**

"When you're playing for the national championship, it's not
a matter of life or death. It's more important than that."
—**DUFFY DAUGHERTY**

The man who can drive himself further once the
effort gets painful is the man who will win.
—ROGER BANNISTER

Some people say I have attitude, and maybe I do.
But I think you have to. You have to believe in yourself when
no one else does. That makes you a winner right there.
—VENUS WILLIAMS

When I go out there, I have no pity on my brother.
I am out there to win.
—JOE FRAZIER

You just can't beat the person who never gives up.
—BABE RUTH

During my 18 years I came to bat almost 10,000 times. I struck out
about 1,700 times and walked maybe 1,800 times.
You figure a ballplayer will average about 500 at bats a season.
That means I played seven years without ever hitting the ball.
—MICKEY MANTLE

You've got to get to the stage in life where going for
it is more important than winning or losing.
—ARTHUR ASHE

To uncover your true potential you must first find your own limits
and then you have to have the courage to blow past them.
—PICABO STREET

There's only one way to become a hitter.

Go up to the plate and get mad.

Get mad at yourself and mad at the pitcher.

—TED WILLIAMS

If you train hard, you'll not only be hard, you'll be hard to beat.

—HERSCHEL WALKER

"I don't believe you have to be better than everybody else. I believe
you have to be better than you ever thought you could be."

—KEN VENTURI

Leaders aren't born, they are made. And they are made
just like anything else, through hard work.

—VINCE LOMBARDI

Never break your putter and your driver in
the same round or you're dead.
—GOLFER TOMMY BOLT (KNOWN AS
"TERRIBLE-TEMPERED TOMMY")

•

If you have everything under control, you're not moving fast enough.
—MARIO ANDRETTI

•

Just keep going. Everybody gets better if they keep at it.
—TED WILLIAMS

•

To have long-term success as a coach or in any position
of leadership, you have to be obsessed in some way
—PAT RILEY

The key to any game is to use your strengths and hide your weaknesses.

—PAUL WESTPHAL

•

"When you lose, you're more motivated. When you win, you fail
to see your mistakes and probably no one can tell you anything."

—VENUS WILLIAMS

•

A champion is someone who gets up when he can't.

—JACK DEMPSEY

•

You don't have the game you played last year or last week.
You only have today's game. It may be far from your best,
but that's all you've got. Harden your heart and make the best of it.

—WALTER HAGEN

Chapter Nine

A Word to the Wise

{Proverbs and Other Folk Sayings}

You often meet your fate on the road you take to avoid it.
—FRENCH PROVERB

A word to the wise is sufficient.
—LATIN PROVERB

"To know the road ahead,

ask those coming back."
—CHINESE PROVERB

If you're ridin' ahead of the herd, take a look back

every now and then to make sure it's still there.
—COWBOY WISDOM

When the best leader's work is done the
people say, "We did it ourselves."
—LAO-TZU

•

The gem cannot be polished without friction,
nor man perfected without trials.
—CHINESE PROVERB

•

A candle loses nothing by lighting another candle.
—ITALIAN PROVERB

•

He who allows his day to pass by without practicing
generosity and enjoying life's pleasures is like a
blacksmith's bellows—he breathes but does not live.
—SANSKRIT PROVERB

We don't see things the way they are. We see them the way we are.

—TALMUD

•

The bravest sight in the world is to see a great

man struggling against adversity.

—SENECA

•

I ask not for a lighter burden, but for broader shoulders.

—JEWISH PROVERB

•

Write the bad things that are done to you in sand, but write

the good things that happen to you on a piece of marble.

—ARABIC SAYING

He who excuses himself, accuses himself.

—FRENCH PROVERB

Never miss a good chance to shut up.

—COWBOY WISDOM

Lower your voice and strengthen your argument.

—LEBANESE PROVERB

Learning is a treasure which accompanies its owner everywhere.

—CHINESE PROVERB

It doesn't matter how slow you go, as long as you don't stop.

—CONFUCIUS

The greater the difficulty, the more glory in surmounting it.
Skillful pilots gain their reputation from storms and tempests.

—EPICETUS

Fall seven times, stand up eight.

—JAPANESE PROVERB

Words that soak into your ears are whispered . . . not yelled.

—COWBOY WISDOM

"Only your real friends will tell you when your face is dirty."
—SICILIAN PROVERB

An ounce of patience is worth a pound of brains.
—DUTCH PROVERB

It is better to be a coward for a minute than
dead for the rest of your life.
—IRISH PROVERB

Not the cry, but the flight of a wild duck,
leads the flock to fly and follow.
—CHINESE PROVERB

Time and Patience would bring the snail to Jerusalem.
—IRISH PROVERB

"If you want to give God a good laugh, tell Him your plans."
—YIDDISH PROVERB

Tell God the truth, but give the judge money.
—RUSSIAN PROVERB

He who wants a rose must respect the thorn.
—PERSIAN PROVERB

No matter how far you have gone on the wrong road, turn back.
— TURKISH PROVERB

Prosperity makes friends, adversity tries them.
— PUBLILIUS SYRUS

Beginning is easy; continuing is hard.
— JAPANESE PROVERB

Life is an echo; what you send out comes back.
— CHINESE PROVERB

When you give a lesson in meanness to a critter or a
person, don't be surprised if they learn their lesson.
—**COWBOY WISDOM**

•

When you shoot an arrow of truth, dip its point in honey.
—**ARABIAN PROVERB**

•

Even nectar is poison if taken in excess.
—**HINDU PROVERB**

•

"Grasp all, lose all."
—**ITALIAN PROVERB**

If you want happiness for an hour, take a nap.

If you want happiness for a day, go fishing.

If you want happiness for a year, inherit a fortune.

If you want happiness for a lifetime, help somebody.

—CHINESE PROVERB

When you are an anvil, be patient; when a hammer, strike.

—ARABIAN PROVERB

How beautiful it is to do nothing, and then rest afterward.

—SPANISH PROVERB

Better a lean agreement than a fat lawsuit.

—YIDDISH PROVERB

Beware the person with nothing to lose.

—ITALIAN PROVERB

"When you're throwin' your weight around, be ready
to have it thrown around by somebody else."

—COWBOY WISDOM

Deal with the faults of others as gently as your own.

—CHINESE PROVERB

"Don't bet more than you can afford to lose."
—SPANISH PROVERB

•

Who goes a-borrowing, goes a-sorrowing.
—ENGLISH PROVERB

•

Better give a penny than lend twenty.
—ITALIAN PROVERB

•

Giving alms never lessens the purse.
—SPANISH PROVERB

Better to go to bed hungry than to wake up in debt.

—RUSSIAN PROVERB

"If you get a reputation as an early riser, you can sleep till noon."

—IRISH PROVERB

If you want your dreams to come true, don't sleep.

—YIDDISH PROVERB

"The quickest way to double your money is to fold
it over and put it back in your pocket."
—COWBOY WISDOM

When the fox preaches, take care of your geese.
—FRENCH PROVERB

If a man is as wise as a serpent, he can afford
to be as harmless as a dove.
—CHEYENNE PROVERB

Surrounding yourself with dwarfs does not make you a giant.

—YIDDISH PROVERB

If you get to thinkin' you're a person of some influence,

try orderin' somebody else's dog around.

—COWBOY WISDOM

Don't be afraid to cry. It will free your mind of sorrowful thoughts.

—HOPI SAYING

Ask about your neighbors, then buy the house.
—YIDDISH PROVERB

You'll never plow a field by turning it over in your mind.
—IRISH PROVERB

Life is simpler when you plow around the stump.
—COWBOY WISDOM

"Beware of still water, a still dog, and a still enemy."
—**YIDDISH PROVERB**

Always drink upstream from the herd.
—**COWBOY WISDOM**

Never rely on the glory of the morning nor
the smiles of your mother-in-law.
—**JAPANESE PROVERB**

"Don't judge a man by the words of his mother;

listen to the comments of his neighbors."

—YIDDISH PROVERB

Fall seven times, stand up eight.

—JAPANESE PROVERB

If you find yourself in a hole, the first thing to do is stop diggin'.

—COWBOY WISDOM

"It's no use carrying an umbrella if your shoes are leaking."

—IRISH PROVERB

When you meet a man, you judge him by his clothes;

when you leave, you judge him by his heart.

—RUSSIAN PROVERB

When the character of a man is not clear to you, look at his friends.

—JAPANESE PROVERB

"Confide a secret to a dumb man and he will speak."

—RUSSIAN PROVERB

Remember that silence is sometimes the best answer.

—COWBOY WISDOM

Give neither counsel nor salt till you are asked for it.
—ITALIAN PROVERB

Lettin' the cat outta the bag is a lot easier 'n puttin' it back in!
—COWBOY WISDOM

"Habits are at first cobwebs, then cables."
—SPANISH PROVERB

"Meanness don't jes' happen overnight."
—COWBOY WISDOM

If you chase two rabbits, both will escape.

—SPANISH PROVERB

"To run away is not glorious, but very healthy."

—RUSSIAN PROVERB

Live a good, honorable life. Then when you get older and

think back, you'll get to enjoy it a second time.

—COWBOY WISDOM

If three people say you are an ass, put on a bridle.

—SPANISH PROVERB

Never approach a bull from the front, a horse from
the rear, or a fool from any direction.
—COWBOY WISDOM

Do not tell the man carrying you that he stinks.
—SIERRA LEONE PROVERB

Only a fool tests the depth of the water with both feet.
—AFRICAN PROVERB

Tell me and I'll forget. Show me, and I may not
remember. Involve me, and I'll understand.
—NATIVE AMERICAN PROVERB

•

The best sermons are lived, not preached.
—COWBOY WISDOM

•

"Remember that your children are not your own,
but are lent to you by the Creator."
—MOHAWK PROVERB

He who would do great things should not attempt them all alone.
—SENECA PROVERB

Seek wisdom, not knowledge. Knowledge is
of the past. Wisdom is of the future.
—LUMBEE PROVERB

"Good judgment comes from experience. The problem
is, a lot of experience comes from bad judgment."
—COWBOY WISDOM

Avoid a friend who covers you with his wings

and destroys you with his beak.

—SPANISH PROVERB

"Cherish youth, but trust old age."

—PUEBLO PROVERB

Don't let yesterday use up too much of today.

—CHEROKEE PROVERB

One is never too old to yearn.

—ITALIAN PROVERB

Timing has a lot to do with the outcome of a rain dance.

—COWBOY WISDOM

"Better is the smoke of one's own house than the fire of another's."

—SPANISH PROVERB

If you look to others for fulfillment, you will never be fulfilled. If your happiness depends on money, you will never be happy with yourself. Be content with what you have; rejoice in the way things are. When you realize there is nothing lacking, the world belongs to you.

—LAO TZU

Take only what you need and leave the land as you found it.
—ARAPAHO PROVERB

What goes around, comes around.
—ANONYMOUS

With lies you may go ahead in the world, but you can never go back.
—RUSSIAN PROVERB

"Don't squat with your spurs on."
—COWBOY WISDOM

Chapter Ten

Enjoy Your Ice Cream

{Advice on Advice}

When we honestly ask ourselves which person in our lives means
the most to us, we often find that it is those who, instead of
giving advice, solutions, or cures, have chosen rather to share
our pain and touch our wounds with a warm and tender hand.

—HENRI NOUWEN

My advice to you is not to inquire why or whither, but just enjoy
your ice cream while it's on your plate—that's my philosophy.

—THORNTON WILDER

The true secret of giving advice is, after you have honestly
given it, to be perfectly indifferent whether it is taken or
not, and never persist in trying to set people right.

—HANNAH WHITALL SMITH

"I always advise people never to give advice."

—**P. G. WODEHOUSE**

•

Seek ye counsel of the aged, for their eyes have looked on the faces
of the years and their ears have hearkened to the voices of Life.
Even if their counsel is displeasing to you, pay heed to them.

—**KAHLIL GIBRAN**

•

When a man comes to me for advice, I find out the
kind of advice he wants, and I give it to him.

—**JOSH BILLINGS**

•

Good advice is something a man gives when
he is too old to set a bad example.

—**FRANÇOIS DE LA ROCHEFOUCAULD**

All you teenagers out there. The big mistake you're making is that
you listen to all that bad advice from kids your own age. You should
listen to your parents. They're entitled to give you bad advice.
—**GEORGE BURNS**

Write down the advice of him who loves you,
though you like it not at present.
—**ITALIAN PROVERB**

The best advice I can give is to ignore advice.
Life is too short to be distracted by the opinions of others.
—**RUSSELL EDSON**

Best advice on writing I've ever received: Finish.
—**PETER MAYLE**

"I have found the best way to give advice to your children is
to find out what they want and then advise them to do it."
—**HARRY S. TRUMAN**

If it's free, it's advice; if you pay for it, it's counseling;
if you can use either one, it's a miracle.
—**JACK ADAMS**

Advice is seldom welcome; and those who want
it the most always like it the least.
—LORD CHESTERFIELD

Advice would always be more acceptable if
it didn't conflict with our plans.
—NEW ENGLAND PROVERB

"Don't take a butcher's advice on how to cook
meat. If he knew, he'd be a chef."
—ANDY ROONEY

"Ask advice only of your equals."

—DANISH PROVERB

Never take the advice of someone who has

not had your kind of trouble.

—SIDNEY J. HARRIS

In giving advice, seek to help, not please, your friend.

—SOLON

People who ask our advice almost never take it. Yet
we should never refuse to give it, upon request, for it
often helps us to see our own way more clearly.
—BRENDAN FRANCIS

The advice of friends must be received with a judicious
reserve; we must not give ourselves up to it and
follow it blindly, whether right or wrong.
—PIERRE CHARRON

I owe my success to having listened respectfully to the very best
advice, and then going away and doing the exact opposite.
—GILBERT K. CHESTERTON

The worst men often give the best advice.
—**PHILIP JAMES BAILEY**

"To profit from good advice requires more wisdom than to give it."
—**JOHN CHURTON COLLINS**

Give advice to learn from your own hidden wisdom.
—**DUANE ALAN HAHN**

A good scare is worth more than good advice.

—HORACE

No vice is so bad as advice.

—MARIE DRESSLER

"When you encounter seemingly good advice that contradicts

other seemingly good advice, ignore them both."

—AL FRANKEN

SELECTED QUOTED SOURCES

Aaron, Henry "Hank" (b. 1934), American baseball player

Abdul-Jabbar, Kareem (b. 1947), American basketball player

Acheson, Dean (1893–1971), U.S. Secretary of State

Acton, John Dalberg-Acton, Lord (1834–1902), British historian

Acuff, Roy (1903–1992), American country music singer

Adams, Franklin P. (1881–1960), American newspaper columnist

Adams, Jack (1895–1968), Canadian ice hockey player

Adams, Joey (1911–1999), American comedian

Adams, John (1735–1826), second U.S. president

Adams, John Quincy (1767–1848), sixth U.S. president

Adams, Scott (b. 1957), American cartoonist; creator of *Dilbert*

Addair, George (1823–1899), American businessman

Addison, Joseph (1672–1719), British essayist

Aesop (620–560 BC), Greek fable author

Affleck, Ben (b. 1972), American actor

Agassi, Andre (b. 1970), American tennis player

Aiken, Howard (1900–1973), American pioneer in computer development

Alcott, Louisa May (1832–1888), American novelist

Alda, Alan (b. 1936), American actor and political activist

Alexander the Great (356 BC–232 BC), King of Macedonia

Algren, Nelson (1909–1981), American novelist

Ali, Muhammad (b. 1942), American prizefighter

Allen, Marcus (b. 1960), American football player

Allen, Richie (b. 1942), American baseball player

Allende, Isabelle (b. 1942), Chilean author

Allston, Washington (1779–1843), American poet and painter

Ambrose, Stephen (1936–2002), American historian

Andrés, José (b. 1969), Spanish restaurateur and chef

Andretti, Mario (b. 1940), American race car driver

Angelou, Maya (b. 1928), American poet, actress, and civil rights activist

Annan, Kofi (b. 1938), Ghanaian diplomat; U.N. secretary general

Annenberg, Walter (1908–2002), American publisher and philanthropist

Anthony, Robert (1916–2006), American management expert

Aristophanes (448–380 BC), Greek dramatist

Aristotle (384–322 BC), Greek philosopher

Arnold, Matthew (1822–1888), British poet

Ash, Mary Kay (1918–2001), American businesswoman

Ashe, Arthur (1943–1993), American tennis player

Asimov, Isaac (1920–1992), American science fiction author

Astor, Nancy, Lady (1879–1964), British legislator and hostess

Auden, W. H. (1907–1973), English-American poet

Auerbach, Arnold "Red" (b. 1917), American basketball coach and executive

Aurelius, Marcus (AD 121–180), Roman emperor and philosopher

Austen, Jane (1775–1817), British novelist

Bach, Johann Sebastian (1685–1750), German composer

Bacon, Sir Francis (1561–1626), British essayist and philosopher

Baden-Powell, Sir Robert (1857–1941), British founder of the Boy Scouts

Bailey, Pearl (1918–1990), American actress and singer

Bailey, Philip James (1816–1902), British poet

Baker, Russell (b. 1925), American writer

Baldwin, James (1924–1987), American author

Ball, Lucille (1911–1989), American actress

Baltasar, Gracian (1601–1658), Spanish philosopher

Banks, Ernie (b. 1931), American baseball player

Bannister, Roger (b. 1929), British track athlete; first man to run a four-minute mile

Barry, Dave (b. 1947), American humor columnist

Barrymore, Ethel (1879–1959), American actress

Beerbohm, Max (1872–1956), British author

Behan, Brendan (1923–1964), Irish playwright and short story author

Bell, Alexander Graham (1847–1922), Scottish scientist and inventor

Bellamy, Carol (b. 1942), American politician and UNICEF director

Bergman, Ingrid (1915–1982), Swedish actress

Berra, Lawrence "Yogi" (1925–2015), American baseball player

Billings, Josh (1818–1885), American humor essayist

Bird, Larry (b. 1956), American basketball player and coach

Blake, William (1757–1827), British poet

Bloomberg, Michael R. (b. 1942), American businessman and politician

Boetcker, William J. H. (1873–1962), American religious leader
Bolt, Tommy (1916–2008), American golfer
Bombeck, Erma (1927–1996), American author and columnist
Bonaparte, Napoleon (1769–1821), French emperor and general
Bono (b. 1960), Irish singer-songwriter
Booth, Shirley (1898–1992), American actress
Borg, Bjorn (b. 1956), Swedish tennis player
Borge, Victor (1909–2000), Danish-American musical entertainer
Bose, Amar Gopal (b. 1929), Indian American electrical engineer
Brackett, Leigh (1915–1978), American novelist and screenwriter
Bradley, Bill (b. 1943), American basketball layer and politician
Bradshaw, Terry (b. 1948), American football player, commentator
Branson, Richard (b. 1950), English businessman
Brock, Lou (b. 1939), American baseball player
Brooks, Herb (1937–2003), American hockey coach
Brothers, Dr. Joyce (b. 1928), American psychologist and columnist
Brown, Les (b. 1945), American author and motivational speaker
Brown, Paul (1908–1991), American football coach
Brown, Rita Mae (b. 1944), American author and social activist
Buck, Pearl (1892–1973), American author
Buddha, Siddhartha Gautama (563–483 BC), Indian philosopher
Buffett, Warren (b. 1930), American businessman
Bulwer-Lytton, Edward (1803–1873), British novelist
Burns, George (1896–1996), American comedian and actor
Buscaglia, Leo (1924–1998), American psychology author

Bush, Barbara (b. 1925), U.S. First Lady; wife of President George H.
Bush and mother of President George W. Bush

Butler, Samuel (1835–1902), British author

Buttons, Red (b. 1919), American comedian and actor

Cameron, James (b. 1954), Canadian filmmaker

Campbell, Joseph (1904–1987), American mythologist

Campbell, Mrs. Patrick (1865–1940), British actress

Camus, Albert (1913–1960), French philosopher and author

Canfield, Jack (b. 1944), American motivational speaker

Capone, Al (1899–1947), American racketeer

Carlin, George (1937–2008), American comedian, actor

Carlyle, Thomas (1795–1881), British historian

Carnegie, Andrew (1835–1919), Scottish-American industrialist

Carnegie, Dale (1888–1955), American motivational speaker and
author

Carson, Rachel (1907–1964), American ecologist and author

Carter, Hodding, III (b. 1935), American politician

Carver, George Washington (1864?–1943), American botanist

Carville, James (b. 1944), American political consultant and
commentator

Castiglione, Baldassare (1478–1529), Italian author and diplomat

Castro, Fidel (b. 1926), premier of Cuba

Cezanne, Paul (1839–1906), French artist

Chan, Francis (b. 1967), American preacher

Chandler, Raymond (1888–1959), American crime fiction author

Chanel, Coco (1883–1971), French fashion designer

Chaplin, Charles "Charlie" (1889–1977), British comic actor

Charron, Pierre (1541–1603), French philosopher

Chekhov, Anton (1860–1904), Russian author

Chesterfield, Philip Stanhope, Earl of (1694–1773), British statesman and author

Chesterton, Gilbert K. (1874–1936), British author

Child, Julia (1912–2004), American chef and author

Chopra, Deepak (b. 1947), American speaker, alternative medicine proponent

Chopra, Priyanka (b. 1982), Indian actress, philanthropist

Christie, Agatha (1890–1976), British crime fiction author

Churchill, Sir Winston (1874–1965), British statesman and author

Cleese, John (b. 1939), British comedian and actor

Clemens, Samuel. *See* Mark Twain

Clooney, George (b. 1961), American actor

Cohan, George M. (1878–1942), American songwriter, playwright, and entertainer

Colbert, Stephen (b. 1964), American comedian

Collins, John Churton (1848–1908), British literary critic

Confucius (551–479 BC), Chinese philosopher and reformer

Conrad, Joseph (1857–1924), Polish-British novelist

Cousins, Norman (1915–1990), American magazine editor and essayist

Covey, Stephen R. (1932–2012), American educator and businessman

Crockett, Davy (1786–1836), American King of the Wild Frontier

Crystal, Billy (b. 1948), American comedian

cummings, e e (1894–1962), American poet, essayist

Currie, Edwina (1946), British member of Parliament

Dali, Salvador (1904–1989), Spanish painter

Damon, Matt (b.1970), American film actor

Daugherty, Duffy (1915–1987), American football coach

da Vinci, Leonardo (1452–1519), Italian artist, inventor, and
     engineer

Davis, Bette (1908–1989), American film actress

de Montaigne, Michel (1533–1592), French essayist and humanist

Dempsey, Jack (1895–1983), American prizefighter

Diana, Princess of Wales (1961–1997), British royal celebrity

Dickens, Charles (1812–1870), British novelist

Dillard, Annie (b. 1945), American author

Diller, Phyllis (b. 1917), American comedian

Disney, Walt (1901–1966), American film animator and producer

Dostoevsky, Fyodor (1821–1881), Russian writer, philosopher

Dressler, Marie (1868–1934), Canadian actress

Drucker, Peter F. (1909–2005), American business author and
     economist

Edelman, Marian Wright (b. 1939), American lawyer and civil rights
     advocate

Edison, Thomas (1847–1931), American inventor and businessman

Edson, Russell (b. 1935), American poet

Einstein, Albert (1879–1955), German physicist

Eisenhower, Dwight D. (1890–1969), thirty-fourth U.S. president

Eliot, T. S. (1888–1965), American-British playwright, poet, and
essayist

Elizabeth II (b. 1926), British monarch

Ellington, Duke (1899–1974) American songwriter, pianist,
conductor

Emerson, Ralph Waldo (1803–1882), American philosopher and poet

Epictetus (AD 55–135), Greek philosopher

Epicurus (341–270 BC), Greek philosopher

Evert, Chris (b. 1954), American tennis player

Feinstein, Dianne (b. 1933), U.S. senator

Feirstein, Bruce (b. 1956), American screenwriter

Fierstein, Harvey (b. 1954), American actor, playwright

Ferber, Edna (1885–1968), American novelist and screenwriter

Fields, W. C. (1880–1946), American comic actor

Fisher, Dorothy Canfield (1879–1958), American author

Fitzgerald, Ella (1917–1996), American jazz singer

Fleming, Peggy (b. 1948), American figure skater

Fonteyn, Margot (1919–1991), British ballet dancer

Forbes, Malcolm (1919–1990), American magazine publisher

Forbes, Victor Ford, Henry (1863–1947), American industrialist

France, Anatole (1844–1924), French novelist and short story author

Francis of Assisi, Saint (1182–1226), Italian cleric and patron saint of
animals

Frank, Anne (1929–1945), German diarist

Franken, Al (b. 1951), American humorist, author, and radio
personality

Franklin, Benjamin (1706–1790), American statesman and author

Frazier, Joe (1944–2011), American boxer

Fromm, Erich (1900–1980), German psychologist and philosopher

Frost, Robert (1874–1963), American poet

Fuller, Buckminster (1895–1983), American architect

Fuller, Margaret (1810–1850), American journalist and women's rights activist

Gable, Dan (b. 1948), American athlete, coach

Galbraith, John Kenneth (1908–2006), American economist

Gandhi, Indira (1917–1984), Indian stateswoman

Gandhi, Mohandas (1869–1948), Indian political and spiritual leader

Gates, Bill (b. 1955), American computer software entrepreneur

Ghosn, Carlos (b. 1954), Brazilian businessman

Gibbons, James Cardinal (1834–1921), Roman Catholic Archbishop of Baltimore

Gibran, Kahlil (1883–1931), Lebanese poet and artist

Goldwyn, Samuel (1882–1974), American movie producer

Gray, Farrah (b. 1984), American businessman

Greeley, Horace (1811–1872), American newspaper editor

Green, Celia (b. 1935), British intellectual and author

Gretzky, Wayne (b. 1961), Canadian ice hockey player and coach

Griffin, Archie (b. 1954), American football player

Groening, Matt (b.1954), American cartoonist, creator of *The Simpsons* television series

Hackett, Buddy (1924–2003), American comedian and actor

Hagen, Walter (1892–1969), American golfer

Hale, Edward Everett (1822–1909), American clergyman and author

Hamm, Mia (b. 1972), American soccer player

Hanh, Thich Nhat (b. 1926), Vietnamese monk

Hawthorne, Nathaniel (1804–1864), American writer

Hayes, Helen (1900–1993), American actress

Hazlitt, William (1778–1830), British critic and essayist

Hein, Piet (1905–1996), Danish scientist and poet

Hemingway, Ernest (1899–1961), American author

Hepburn, Katharine (1907–2003), American stage and film actress

Hesburgh, Theodore M., Father (b. 1917), American cleric and academic

Hesse, Herman (1877–1962), German poet, novelist

Hirsch, Samson (1808–1888), German rabbi

Holtz, Lou (b. 1937), American football coach

Hopper, Grace (1906–1992), American naval officer and computer developer

Horace (65–8 BC), Roman poet

Hsieh, Tony (b. 1973), American internet entrepreneur

Hubbard, Elbert (1856–1915), American author

Hubbard, Kin [Frank McKinney] (1868–1930), American cartoonist, humorist, and journalist

Hughes, Charles Evans (1862–1948), Chief Justice of U.S. Supreme Court

Hughes, Robert (1938–2012), Australian art critic writer

Huxley, Aldous (1894–1963), British author

Huxley, Thomas Henry (1825–1895), British biologist and philosopher

Iacocca, Lee (b. 1934), American automobile executive

Ibsen, Henrik (1828–1906), Norwegian dramatist

Jackson, Jesse (b. 1941), American civil rights leader and politician

James, William (1842–1910), American philosopher

Jefferson, Thomas (1743–1826), third U.S. president

Jessell, George (1898–1981), American comedian

Jeter, Derek (b. 1974), American baseball player

Jobs, Steven (b. 1955–2011), American computer entrepreneur

Johnson, Earvin "Magic" (b. 1959), American basketball player

Johnson, Samuel (1709–1784), British author

Jones, Bobby (1902–1971), American golfer

Jong, Erica (b. 1942), American author

Joplin, Janis (1943–1970), American pop singer

Jordan, Michael (b. 1963), American basketball player

Joyner-Kersee, Jackie (b. 1962), American track and field athlete

Kafka, Franz (1883–1924), Czech author

Kaiser, Henry J. (1882–1967), American industrialist

Kasdan, Lawrence (b. 1949), American screenwriter and producer

Kaufman, George S. (1889–1961), American playwright, director, and journalist

Kaufman, Margo (1954–2000), American columnist

Keller, Helen (1880–1968), American author, activist, and lecturer

Kennedy, Florynce (b. 1916), American civil rights leader

Kennedy, John Fitzgerald (1917–1963), thirty-fifth U.S. president

Kennedy, Robert F. (1925–1968), U.S. senator and attorney general

Kettering, Charles F. (1876–1958), American inventor

Khan, Salman (b. 1965), Indian actor

Killy, Jean-Claude (b. 1943), French skier

Kimbrough, Emily (1899–1989), American author and editor

King, Billie Jean (b. 1943), American tennis player

King Jr., Martin Luther (1929–1968), American minister and civil rights activist

Kingsley, Charles (1819–1875), British novelist and clergyman

Kingsolver, Barbara (b. 1955), American novelist

Knight, Ray (b. 1952), American baseball player

Koontz, Dean (b. 1945), American novelist

Kroc, Ray (1902–1984), American businessman, developer of McDonald's

Lamarr, Hedy (1914–2000), Austrian-American actress and inventor

Landers, Ann [Esther Lederer] (1918–2002), American newspaper advice columnist

Lao-tzu (4th century BC), Chinese Taoist philosopher

Larson, Doug (b. 1926), American newspaper columnist

Le Guin, Ursula K. (b. 1929), American author

Lec, Stanislaw Jerzy (1909–1966), Polish poet

Lee, Bruce(1940–1973), Hong Kong American actor, martial arts specialist

Lehman, Herbert (1878–1963), American politician

Leunig, Michael (b. 1945), Australian political cartoonist

Levenson, Sam (1911–1980), American humorist

Lewis, John (b. 1940), American civil rights activist, congressman

Lichtenberg, Georg C. (1742–1799), German physicist and author

Lincoln, Abraham (1809–1865), sixteenth American president

Lombardi, Vince (1913–1970), American football coach

London, Jack (1876–1916), American author

Longfellow, Henry Wadsworth (1807–1882), American poet

Lorimer, George Horace (1868–1937), American magazine editor

Madden, John (b. 1936), American football coach, commentator

Mahfouz, Naguib (1911–2006), Egyptian novelist

Maimonides, Moses (1135–1204), Spanish-Jewish philosopher and
physician

Maitreya (b. 1944), Persian religious leader

Mantle, Mickey (1931–1995), American baseball player

Marshall, George C. (1880–1959), American general and statesman

Martin, Judith [Miss Manners] (b. 1938), American etiquette expert

Martin, Steve (b. 1945), American comedian, writer, producer, and
actor

Marx, Groucho (Julius) (1890–1977), American humorist

Matthau, Walter (1920–2000), American actor

Maugham, W. Somerset (1874–1965), British novelist, playwright,
and short story author

Maurois, André (1885–1967), French author

Mayle, Peter (b. 1939), British author

McGraw, Dr. Phil (b. 1950), American television personality

Mencken, Henry L[ouis] (1880–1956), American editor and critic

Menninger, William C. (1899–1966), American physician and
entrepreneur

Milne, A. A. (1882–1956), British author

Mingus, Charles (1922–1979), American jazz musician

Mitchell, Maria (1818–1889), American astronomer

Miyazawa, Kenji (1896–1933), Japanese poet

Mizner, Wilson (1876–1933), American screenwriter

Molière, Jean-Baptiste (1622–1673), French dramatist

Monroe, Marilyn (1926–1962), American actress

Montessori, Maria (1870–1952), Italian educator and physician

Montgomery, L. M. (1874–1942), Canadian author

Moore, Michael (b. 1954), American documentary filmmaker

Morgan, John Pierpont (1837–1913), American financier

Morley, Christopher (1890–1957), American poet, novelist, and
journalist

Morita, Akio (1921–1999), Japanese businessman

Munro, H[ector] H[ugh] [pen name Saki] (1870–1916), British author

Nader, Ralph (b. 1934), American activist, author

Nash, Ogden (1902–1971), American poet

Niebuhr, Dr. Reinhold (1892–1971), German theologian

Nin, Anaïs (1903–1977), French-American author

Nixon, Richard (1913–1994), thirty-seventh U.S. president

O'Brien, Conan (b. 1963), American humorist, television host

Obama, Barack, (b. 1961), American politician, forty-fourth U.S.
president

Onassis, Aristotle (1900–1975), Greek businessman

Osmond, Marie (b. 1959), American entertainer

Ovid (43 BC–AD 17), Roman poet

Paige, Leroy "Satchel" (1906–1982), American baseball player

Palmer, Arnold (b. 1929), American golfer

Patton, George S. (1885–1945), U.S. Army general in World War II

Peale, Norman Vincent (1898–1993), American minister and author

Peale, Ruth Stafford (1906–2008), American religious author and speaker

Pele (Edson Arantes do Nascimento) (b. 1940), Brazilian soccer player

Penney, J. C. (1875–1971), American businessman and entrepreneur

Peters, Tom (b. 1942), American business management guru

Plath, Sylvia (1932–1963), American poet

Plato (427–347 BC), Greek philosopher

Pope, Alexander (1688–1744), British poet and satirist

Post, Emily (1873–1960), American etiquette authority

Powell, Colin (b. 1937), American diplomat, general

Presley, Elvis, (1935–1977), American entertainer

Price, Leontyne (b. 1927), American opera singer

Prudden, Bonnie (b. 1914), American rock climber

Rand, Ayn (1905–1982), Russian-American philosopher and author

Raymond, Eric S. (b. 1957), American author

Repplier, Agnes (1858–1950), American essayist

Richards, Keith (b. 1943), British rock musician

Rickey, Branch (1881–1965), American baseball executive

Rilke, Rainer Maria (1875–1926), Austrian author

Rivera, Chita (b. 1933), American actress and dancer

Robbins, Anthony (b. 1960), American motivational speaker and author

Rockefeller, John D. (1839–1937), American business magnate, philanthropist

Rockne, Knute (1888–1931), American football coach

Rogers, Fred [Mr. Rogers] (1928–2003), American television personality

Rogers, Will (1879–1935), American humorist and performer

Rohn, Jim (b. 1931), American motivational speaker and author

Rooney, Andy (b. 1919), American columnist and television commentator

Roosevelt, Eleanor (1884–1962), U.S. First Lady and diplomat

Roosevelt, Theodore (1858–1919), twenty-sixth U.S. president

Rowling, J. K. (b. 1965), British writer, best known for *Harry Potter*

Royce, Henry (1863–1933), British pioneering car manufacturer

Rumi (1207–1273), Persian poet

Runyon, Damon (1884–1946), American author and journalist

Ruskin, John (1819–1900), British author, artist, and poet

Russell, Bertrand (1872–1970), British logician, philosopher, and mathematician

Ruth, George Herman "Babe" (1895–1948), American baseball player

Ryun, Jim (b. 1947), American miler

Saadi (1184–1283/1291?), Persian poet

Saki. *See* H. H. Munro

Sandberg, Sheryl (b. 1969), American technology expert

Santayana, George (1863–1952), Spanish philosopher, essayist, poet, and novelist

Sartre, Jean-Paul (1905–1980), French philosopher

Schuller, Robert (1936–2015), American evangelist

Schulz, Charles (1922–2000), American cartoonist; creator of *Peanuts*

Schwarzenegger, Arnold (b. 1947), Austrian American actor, politician

Schweitzer, Albert (1875–1965), German physician, musician, and theologian

Seger, Bob (b. 1945), American musician

Seneca, Lucius Annaeus (4 BC–AD 65), Roman philosopher, statesman, and dramatist

Seuss, Dr. [pseudonym of Theodore Seuss Geisel] (1904–1991), American children's books author and illustrator

Shakespeare, William (1564–1616), British dramatist

Shaw, George Bernard (1856–1950), Irish dramatist and critic

Shaw, Henry Wheeler. *See* Josh Billings

Shepard, Dax (b. 1975), American actor, director

Sherman, Bobby (b.1943), American pop singer and actor

Shoemaker, Bill (1931–2003), American jockey

Sibelius, Jean (1865–1957), Finnish composer

Smiley, Jane (b. 1949), American novelist

Smith, Hannah Whitall (1832–1911), American Christian mystic and suffragette

Smith, Liz (b. 1923), American author and journalist

Smith, Logan Pearsall (1865–1946), American essayist

Smith, Sydney (1771–1845), British author and clergyman

Smith, Will (b. 1968), American actor

Socrates (c. 470–399 BC), Greek philosopher

Solon (c. 638–558 BC), Greek statesman and poet

Sotomayor, Sonia (b. 1954), Associate Justice of the U.S. Supreme Court

Steele, Tommy (b. 1936), British pop singer

Steinbeck, John (1902–1968), American novelist and screenwriter

Stewart, Jon (b. 1962), American television personality

Swanson, Claude (1862–1939), American lawyer and politician

Sweetland, Ben (n.d.), American psychologist, author

Swift, Jonathan (1667–1745), British author and satirist

Tagore, Rabindranath (1861–1941), Indian poet, philosopher, author, and dramatist

Tennyson, Alfred, Lord (1809–1892), British poet

Tenzin, Gyatso (b. 1935), Tibetan fourteenth Dalai Lama

Teresa, Mother (1910–1997), Albanian-Indian nun and social activist

Theismann, Joe (b. 1949), American football player

Thompson, Hunter S. (1937–2005), American journalist

Thoreau, Henry David (1817–1862), American author, naturalist, and philosopher

Thurber, James (1894–1961), American humorist

Tillich, Paul (1886–1965), German theologian and philosopher

Todd, Mike (1907 or 1909–1958), American movie producer

Truman, Harry S. (1884–1972), thirty-third U.S. president

Tse-tung, Mao (1893–1976), Chinese leader

Turner, Tina (b. 1939), American pop singer

Twain, Mark [pen name of Samuel L. Clemens] (1835–1910), American humorist and author

Updike, John (1932–2009), American novelist

Valvano, Jim (1946–1993), American basketball coach

Van Buren, Abigail [pseudonym of Pauline and Jeanne Phillips], American newspaper advice columnists

Vanderbilt, Amy (1908–1974), American authority on etiquette

van Dyke, Henry (1852–1933), American clergyman, educator, and author

van Gogh, Vincent (1853–1890), Dutch painter

Venturi, Ken (b. 1931), American golfer

von Ebner-Eschenbach, Marie (1830–1916), Austrian author

von Goethe, Johann Wolfgang (1749–1832), German novelist, scientist, and philosopher

Vonnegut, Kurt (1922–2007), American writer

Walker, Herschel (b. 1962), American football player

Washington, Denzel (b. 1952), American actor, director, producer

Washington, George (1732–1799), first U.S. president

Watson, Thomas J. (1874–1956), American businessman, founder of IBM

Watts, Alan (1915–1973), British author and philosopher

Welch, Jack (b.1935), American businessman

West, Cornell (b. 1953), American philosopher, political activist

West, Jessamyn (1902–1984), American author

West, Mae (1892?–1980), American actress

Westheimer, Dr. Ruth (b. 1928), American author and therapist

Westphal, Paul (b. 1950), American basketball player and coach

Wharton, Edith (1863–1967), American novelist, Pulitzer Prize winner

Wiesel, Elie, (1928–2016), Jewish-American writer, professor,
    political activist, Nobel Laureate and Holocaust survivor
Wilcox, Ella Wheeler (1850–1919), American author and poet
Wilde, Oscar (1854–1900), Irish dramatist
Wilder, Thornton (1897–1975), American novelist and playwright
Willkie, Wendell (1892–1944), American politician
Williams, Ted (1918–2002), American baseball player
Williams, Venus (b. 1980), American tennis player
Wilson, Woodrow (1856–1924), twenty-eighth U.S. president
Yousafzai, Malala (b. 1997) Pakistani activist